Halfway up the Tree

Halfway up the Tree

Peter Ustinov

RANDOM HOUSE · NEW YORK

HALFWAY UP THE TREE *was first presented on November 7, 1967, by Alexander H. Cohen at the Brooks Atkinson Theatre in New York City, with the following cast:*

(In order of appearance)

LADY FITZBUTTRESS	Eileen Herlie
HELGA	Hanne Bork
GENERAL SIR MALLALIEU FITZBUTTRESS	Anthony Quayle
ROBERT	Sam Waterston
LESLEY	"Lesley"
JUDY	Margaret Linn
TINY GILLIATT-BROWN	William Larsen
BASIL UTTERWOOD	John Tillinger
THE VICAR	Graham Jarvis

Directed by Peter Ustinov

Associate Producer Hildy Parks

Scenery and Lighting by Ralph Alswang

Production Supervisor Jerry Adler

Costumes by James Hart Stearns

Act One

The interior of a cottage, somewhere near the great military retirement area near Fleet, in Hampshire, England. LADY FITZBUTTRESS *is melancholy as she opens yet another letter, and puts it aside. She sighs.* HELGA, *the ravishing Norwegian au-pair, enters, dressed to go out. She is full of solicitude.*

HELGA   What's the matter, madame?

LADY   Nothing, Helga. (*With determination*) Nothing.

HELGA   Oh yes, there is something, I can see it.

LADY (*Smiling bravely*)   You shouldn't be able to, my dear. I'm trying to put a brave face on it.

HELGA   It's no use. We in Scandinavia have learned it long ago. Depression has a value. It spoils it to fight against it. (*Pause*) I have some pills, if you want them.

LADY   Pills? What for?

HELGA   To commit suicide.

LADY   Good gracious, do I look as though I were contemplating suicide?

HELGA (*Earnestly*)   Yes. Don't fight it if you feel that way. It's good for the soul.

3

LADY You're not serious, Helga.

HELGA (*Looking for the pills*) Perfectly. I have done it often. (*She sits on the sofa, stage left*) It is most refreshing.

LADY You're very lucky. There are many people who don't have the opportunity to do it more than once.

HELGA Those are people who do it successfully.

LADY You're a failure, is that it?

HELGA A complete failure.
       (HELGA *gets her coat*)

LADY Have you done the washing up?

HELGA No, not even that. I have to go for my English lesson now.

LADY You speak English perfectly well.

HELGA Yes, but my mother thinks I don't. That's why I'm here.

LADY Does she speak English?

HELGA Not a word.

LADY (*Buttoning* HELGA's *coat*) I see. You're sure she didn't send you abroad because you were committing suicide a little too often?

HELGA   Yes, that's quite true. The neighbors objected.

LADY (*Sighing*)   The neighbors always object, don't they?

HELGA   I hate neighbors. (*Suddenly*) Is that your trouble too?

LADY (*Sharply*)   My trouble is my business.

HELGA   I'm sorry.

LADY   I hope at least you've done your own washing up.

HELGA   No.

LADY   Oh Helga, you know my husband is supposed to return today . . .

HELGA (*Without enthusiasm*)   I know. I'm almost as excited as you are.

LADY   Couldn't you have made the effort today of all days?

HELGA   I could, but I didn't. Isn't that scandalous? I tell you, I'm a complete failure. Am I fired?

LADY (*After a moment*)   No.

HELGA   It's modern youth, you know, madame. We're selfish and lazy. We were born into a world where everything is automatic, and no child alive today can hope to understand the way everything around him works.

5

LADY What do you mean?

HELGA Well, the child of a cave man was like an animal. He had to learn to survive very quickly, otherwise he died. There was no one to help, only instinct. He didn't have to be told his friends and his enemies—he knew them on sight. To be warm, he had to build a fire. To eat, he had to kill. To pass away the time, he had to invent his own amusements. He was lucky.

LADY You would have liked to have been a cave woman?

HELGA Oh, yes.

LADY (*Smiles*) Very well, Helga, off you go. When will you be home?

HELGA You're sure I'm not fired?

LADY Of course not.

HELGA (*Puzzled*) Why not?

LADY You think you ought to be fired?

HELGA Oh yes. You can't be keeping me on because of the work I do.

LADY (*Reasonably*) No.

HELGA Why then?

LADY I think you're decorative. My husband comes back today . . . he's been four years in the jungle. I can no

6

longer furnish the youth and the charm an elderly man requires.

HELGA   Oh . . . You see me as a sort of geisha.

LADY   As a geisha you'd have been sacked long ago. Your tea ceremonies are a disaster, even in the relatively relaxed atmosphere of Hampshire. No, I think you're very amusing . . . and splendidly insubordinate . . . just what a retiring general needs to prove to him that there are delights to civilian life which he may have been forced to overlook. (*The doorbell rings*) Oh, it can't be . . . not yet. Helga, would you mind opening the door?

HELGA   Of course not.
      (*While* HELGA *is out,* LADY FITZBUTTRESS *tidies her hair, and gives evidence of a deep worry which has only been superficially appeased by* HELGA's *conversation. After a moment, the* GENERAL, *a military man of sixty, enters, in civilian clothes, smoking a pipe, with a raincoat over his arm*)

GENERAL   Remember me? General Sir Mallalieu St. John Fitzbuttress, VC, DSO, Legion of Merit, Croix de Guerre. Clubs: Altheneum, Boodles, Cavalry and Pratts. Hobbies: polo, fly-fishing and crossword puzzles.

LADY (*Smiling sweetly but nervously*)   Which is your way of telling me off for not having met you at the station.

GENERAL   Full marks.

LADY   Don't I get a kiss after four years?

7

GENERAL Who's this?

LADY Helga.

GENERAL What happened to old Mrs. Bellenger?

LADY She retired.

GENERAL She wasn't as old as all that, was she?

LADY She was sixty-eight when you left for Malaya. She's now seventy-two.

GENERAL Yes, I suppose that's reasonable.

HELGA May I say something?

GENERAL What is it?

HELGA Welcome home.

GENERAL Oh, that's very good of you. German, are you?

HELGA Norwegian.

GENERAL Norwegian! Ah, don't see many of those about. The land of the fjords and the midnight sun, if my memory serves me.

HELGA That is correct.

GENERAL Damned awkward coastline.

8

HELGA   Many people consider it extremely beautiful.

GENERAL   Only time I was there, I had to evacuate five hundred men under the very noses of the Hun. As I say, damned awkward coastline.

HELGA   And how was Malaya? Whom were you fighting?

GENERAL   The Government, mainly.

HELGA   The Malayan Government?

GENERAL   The British Government.

HELGA   And is it beautiful? Malaya?

GENERAL   I'll say this for it, it's an easier coastline.

HELGA   Oh. That is cause to be thankful. Especially for a General. Now, if you will excuse me . . .

GENERAL   Where are you going?

HELGA   I have an English lesson in two hours' time in London.

GENERAL   You speak English quite adequately.

HELGA   I have a very nice gentleman in London who is teaching me.

LADY   Good-by, Helga. I'll leave your supper in the fridge.

9

HELGA   Thank you, madame. Good-by, sir.

GENERAL   By . . . And skaal . . .
        (HELGA *exits*)

LADY   Well, it's as though you never left, isn't it? No kiss.

GENERAL (*Daydreaming*)   No what?

LADY   Never mind.

GENERAL (*After a pause*)   It's not that I really expected to
be met . . . no, it's not that . . . I just thought some
kind of homecoming . . . the children . . .

LADY   I told them you were returning. They may turn up.

GENERAL   Where are they?

LADY (*Tactful*)   Tubby, a great deal has happened since
you left.

GENERAL (*Thoughtful*)   Tubby. It's always bad news when
you call me by my nickname.

LADY   It's not exactly bad . . . it's different . . . I suppose
we all have to live with the times.

GENERAL   I see nothing to quarrel with in that statement.

LADY   Of course not, it's just that . . . we haven't all been
winkling out Indonesian paratroops in Malaya . . . while

you've been doing that—vital work . . . other things have been happening at home.

GENERAL Well, that's not surprising. First of all, let me tell you the truth. My work out there wasn't vital at all. It was damned idiotic, a waste of my time and my talent.

LADY Oh? The papers said . . .

GENERAL I don't give a rap what the papers said. I know best. I hadn't the men or the equipment to do the job properly—and in any case, the job wasn't worth doing. The dying gasp of a colonial empire has never been an ingratiating sound, and we have not contrived to prove any exception to the rule. I suppose you read my letter to the *Times?*

LADY No.

GENERAL Oh, well, then we're even. We no longer know anything about one another.

LADY I didn't take the *Times* in your absence. I took a cheaper paper.

GENERAL I don't write to cheaper papers. (*Pause*) Very well, old girl. We're not getting anywhere, are we? I can see I'll have to ask you a few direct questions.

LADY You've changed, Tubby.

GENERAL   Have I? Well, I suppose it's from years of cross-examining Communist saboteurs in the jungle. It tends to make a fellow peremptory.

LADY   So long as you don't twist my arm, I think I can put up with it.

GENERAL   I never resorted to that kind of activity unless it was quite clear the fellow didn't intend to answer. Did Robert pass his finals at Oxford?

LADY   No.

GENERAL   Well, there you are. We're getting somewhere at last. Is he going to take another crack at them?

LADY   No. He's no longer there.

GENERAL   Aha. He left, did he?

LADY   He was sent down.

GENERAL   (*Chuckles*)   The lad's got more spunk than I thought. What did he do? Climb some spire or other?

LADY   Oh, if it had only been that.

GENERAL   I'm waiting, Doris.

LADY   (*After a moment of agitation*)   I didn't know how to tell you. I just didn't know how to tell you . . .

GENERAL (*After another moment*) You evidently still don't. Let me help you. He . . . he . . . (*He searches for some possible disgrace*) He raped his tutor's daughter.

LADY (*An echo*) Oh, if it had only been that.

GENERAL (*Quickly*) Good gracious. I confess I've run out of possibilities.

LADY (*With contained agony*) I can only tell you this. I asked in a few friends and neighbors for a little cocktail in your honor.

GENERAL That was thoughtful of you. When? This evening?

LADY Yes. They all refused.

GENERAL Really? Because of Bob?

LADY Oh, they have their troubles too. Young Paul Gilliatt-Brown—you know, his parents had such high hopes in him—he's in prison.

GENERAL Is that where Bob is too?

LADY Oh heavens, no. How could you think such a thing?

GENERAL Now don't you shield the lad, Doris. If he's in prison, I'd like to go and visit him and take him a few sandwiches.

LADY No, no, he's not in prison. He's . . . he's at large.

GENERAL Hiding, is he? Here? Has he taken sanctuary in the attic, is that it? Was he involved in the Great Train Robbery?

LADY Good God, I hope not. I never thought of that.

GENERAL It is a possibility then, is it?

LADY No. No, he'd never have the gumption. He's too much of an idealist.

GENERAL An idealist? Now you are worrying me. My son an idealist. I tell you what. Let's give Robert a rest. Now what about Judy?

LADY Judy! Judy . . . Judy . . .
    (*She wrings her hands*)

GENERAL We haven't any other children to fall back on, you know. (*Tactful*) She's alive, I trust.

LADY (*With point*) Oh yes. Very much so.

GENERAL Right. Now, suppose we start from the beginning, from the time I left. Judy was at school, playing hockey with tremendous abandon.

LADY Well, she's no longer at school.

GENERAL Obviously not. If Mrs. Bellenger is four years older, presumably Judy is also.

LADY I sometimes wonder. Oh, what a trouble she has been to me, that girl. She's like you, with her iron will. She even looks like you.

GENERAL She hasn't grown a mustache, I trust.

LADY Yes, and she's frivolous like you, too. Nothing reaches her. No appeal to reason, no unhappiness in others, no mother's tears . . . (*Suddenly*) I must pull myself together.
(*A door slams*)

GENERAL Steady, old girl. Someone's here, I think. (ROBERT *appears*) Friend of yours, Doris?
(*The door opens and* ROBERT *stands there, his hair down to the small of his back, wearing the paraphernalia of the modern beatnik. He has a guitar slung over his shoulder*)

ROBERT Dad?

GENERAL (*Rising, affectionate*) Robert, I hardly recognized you. My, how you've grown!

ROBERT My hair's grown. I don't think I've grown.

GENERAL That's what I meant. Well, well, well. So we've left Oxford, have we?

ROBERT Not very honorably.

GENERAL Oh, what's the difference. It's only education.

ROBERT   You don't mean that for a moment.

GENERAL   Don't I? Tell me about yourself. Are you earning a living?

ROBERT   Not yet. I'm borrowing.

GENERAL   Borrowing? Money, d'you mean?

ROBERT   No, things mainly. Shoes, underpants, bread.

GENERAL   Combs? Hairbrushes?

ROBERT (*Sheepish*)   No.

GENERAL   I see you haven't managed to borrow any socks yet.

ROBERT   Oh yes, I have, but the holes outgrew them.

GENERAL (*Laughing*)   Damned amusing, that.

ROBERT   It's no use, Dad. I wish you wouldn't try to understand. You never will.

GENERAL   Are you sure?

ROBERT   Positive.

GENERAL   Give me a sporting chance.

ROBERT   Sporting chances don't exist any more.

GENERAL   Give me an unsporting chance then. D'you play that instrument?

ROBERT   It's a guitar.

GENERAL   I may be a General, Bob, but I honestly didn't think for a moment it was a bassoon.

ROBERT   No, I don't play it. I just carry it.

GENERAL   Well, that doesn't seem so extraordinary to me. I sometimes have to carry a sword, but I wouldn't for the life of me know how to use it. It's just part of your uniform, isn't it, old man?

ROBERT   Yes. I suppose it is. My mistress plays quite well.

GENERAL   Your what?

ROBERT   My mistress.

GENERAL   You're married, are you?

ROBERT   No.

GENERAL   I'm sorry. I'm just showing my age. In my day, we only referred to a woman as a mistress when she provided extracurricular joy to a married man. If we were unmarried, we referred to the lady whose bed we were sharing by some such name as girl friend, or even, in extremely sheltered circles, as one's "intended."

LADY   Tubby!

GENERAL   What?

LADY   I've never heard you speak like that!

GENERAL   It's a father's duty to have a few talks with his son when the latter reaches a certain age, Doris. Owing to my absence, these talks never took place. I am rectifying that error.

ROBERT   I'm afraid it's too late, Dad. I really came to say good-by.

GENERAL   What on earth for?

ROBERT   You represent so much which sickens the young people of my generation—there's no possibility of any reconciliation—no desire for it, even. We're strangers.

GENERAL   At least have the generosity to say enemies if you must say something, Bob—but not strangers.

ROBERT   God knows, I don't want to hurt your feelings, Dad. I know you think you've done a lot for me.

GENERAL   I think nothing of the sort. I spent a pleasant night in bed with Mother, and you were the result.

LADY   Mallalieu!

GENERAL   Silence, Doris. I'm being extremely flattering to you, and all you can think of doing is to be shocked. You should be delighted I still remember all that went on in those days. (*To* ROBERT) You owe me nothing. Nothing at all. It is part of the function of a parent to be like a bone to a puppy—he is an object for the child to sharpen his teeth on. If you have sharpened your teeth on me to the extent of wandering around in blue jeans with filthy ankles and with a guitar around your neck you can't even play, that is entirely your affair. If, on top of it all, you have found a girl to share your mattress or park bench with you, I regard it as a personal triumph, and I congratulate you most wholeheartedly. You obviously know what you are doing, and I respect that.

ROBERT   You may respect it, but you don't understand it.

GENERAL   Why should I understand it once I respect it? Isn't that enough?

ROBERT (*With sudden fire*.) No! You won't be so generous with your respect once I tell you why I was sent down from Oxford!

LADY   No, Robert, no!

GENERAL (*Calm*)   Test me.

ROBERT   It was while Sir Arnold Cleaver, the ex-prime minister of Australia, was receiving his honorary degree.

GENERAL   Oh, Cleaver! That awful, old humbug. There's nothing worse than an Australian trying to out-blimp the British.

ROBERT You think that?

GENERAL (*Sharp*) 'Course I think that. I've always thought it. Always will.

ROBERT Well, anyway, I shouted "Ban the bomb! Peace in Vietnam!" during the church service.

LADY (*Suffering*) Oh, Robert.

GENERAL And they sent you down for that? Ridiculous.

ROBERT I wanted to be sent down!

GENERAL That's another matter. I'm talking about them now. First of all, anybody in his right mind wants the bomb banned.

ROBERT (*Hotly*) Even a soldier?

GENERAL Most of all a soldier! Damn thing's taken all the amusement out of war. Secondly, peace in Vietnam. Anyone with a grain of sense wants peace everywhere.

ROBERT But you fought in Malaya, against the legitimate aspiration of its people.

GENERAL And at the request of a corrupt Government, don't forget that. I didn't fight at all. I pottered around in the jungle, and showed willing. I wasted four years of my life and so did everyone else involved.

ROBERT   But did you protest? Did you raise a finger?

GENERAL   No, I didn't, because I had my loyalties.

ROBERT   I have no loyalties. I'm utterly and completely free.

GENERAL   With all due respect, nobody who borrows is completely free.

ROBERT   Freedom is a spiritual force, not a financial one.

GENERAL   Fair enough 'till you can't find anyone to lend you a pair of shoes.

ROBERT   I'm still free to go barefoot.

GENERAL   Why don't you?

ROBERT   Why should I, if I find someone willing to lend me shoes?

GENERAL   That's a good point.

LADY   But to shout out such slogans in church!

GENERAL   Churches are quiet places, Doris. Presumably Bob chose it because it was there that he could be guaranteed a hearing. I would call that sound strategy.

ROBERT   You're only saying that. You're as shocked as Mother is.

GENERAL   I don't necessarily approve your action, Bob. I'm only saying that once you had determined to make such a statement in public, your choice of locale showed courage, initiative and resource. Which is more than can be said for the reaction of the authorities.

ROBERT What would you have done in their place?

GENERAL Me? I'd have ignored you. (ROBERT *makes a sarcastic gesture*) I blame them for giving you a sense of self-importance out of all proportion to the magnitude of your misdemeanor. As usual, the *Times* is a model of how such matters should be handled.

ROBERT (*Ironic*) What did the *Times* say?

GENERAL (*Equally ironic*) The *Times* failed to report it. Now, to turn to more constructive issues. When will we have an opportunity of seeing this mistress of yours?

ROBERT I don't know.

GENERAL Where is she?

ROBERT On the lawn.

GENERAL But it's raining.

ROBERT Is it? Doesn't surprise me. She quite likes the rain.

GENERAL Bring her in—or will that spoil her enjoyment?

ROBERT I don't think she wants to come in.

GENERAL   Ask her. Or d'you want me to go out?

ROBERT   No, no. (*As he goes, he mutters*) There's always such a thing about everyone knowing everyone . . .

LADY (*Tearful*)   Well . . .

GENERAL   Well what?

LADY   Now you know half the worst. I must say, I thought you'd hit the ceiling.

GENERAL   I'm a General, Doris.

LADY   I know that, dear.

GENERAL   Yes, and I wouldn't be a General if I hadn't done reasonably well at Sandhurst and Staff Cottage—and there I was taught never to be taken by surprise. I may be surprised, Doris, but I have not been taken by surprise.
   (ROBERT *enters with a person exactly like him in dress and hairstyle, also carrying a guitar*)

ROBERT   This is Lesley, Dad.

LADY   Hello, Lesley.

LESLEY   Doris.

LADY   That is Robert's father.

GENERAL   I'm over here, my dear.

23

LESLEY   General.

GENERAL   They call me Tubby. (*A moment of awkwardness*) How . . . em . . . where did you two meet?

ROBERT   On the street, wasn't it?

LESLEY   Yeah.

GENERAL   Well, that's as good a place as any. Did you have any mutual friends?

ROBERT   No, we just looked at one another and had a good giggle. (GENERAL *laughs*) What are you laughing at?

GENERAL   I'm joining in the giggle. Is that permitted?

LESLEY   Come on, Bob. Let's go.

ROBERT   Well, good-by now.

GENERAL   Where are you going?

ROBERT   We haven't any fixed plans. I think Lesley just wants to get out of here.

GENERAL   Before you go, could I just have a word with you alone, Bob?

ROBERT   I know what you're going to say.

GENERAL   I bet you don't. Doris, perhaps you could take Lesley and show her your marmalades, or if she'd care to wait out in the rain . . .

LESLEY   It's bad for the guitar.

LADY   Come on, Lesley. Robert won't be long.

ROBERT   I don't have to stay, Les.

LADY   Please, Bob. It's the least you can do. Come on, Lesley.
   (*They exit*)

ROBERT (*Rudely*)   Well?

GENERAL   Bob . . . are you sure that's a girl?

ROBERT   What d'you mean, am I sure?

GENERAL   I mean, are you sure. Have you evidence?

ROBERT   Didn't I say she was my mistress?

GENERAL   Anyone can *say* anything. I am putting my cards on the table, old man.

ROBERT   You're putting my cards on the table, which I resent. You stick to your own cards.

GENERAL   Look here, Bob. It may be that you prefer men. Such things do occur. Even in the best circles—above all in the best circles. A great many of the finest soldiers were that way inclined. It's a fact one has to accept, no questions asked. I'll never bring it up again, but I'd rather know once and for all. Is Lesley a man?

25

ROBERT (*Beside himself*) You enrage me, honestly. What on earth could lead you to imagine that Lesley could possibly be a man?

GENERAL First of all, she has a bass voice.

ROBERT She's a most gifted folk singer.

GENERAL I'm not commenting on the quality of the voice. I'm saying it's a bass voice.

ROBERT It's a deep voice, admittedly.

GENERAL Then, she's flatter in front than you are.

ROBERT She never wears a bra.

GENERAL I've been away for a long time, I know, but I seem to remember that the female breast, whether it is captive and uplifted, or unfettered and pendulous, still has to go somewhere. It's a question of up, down, or round the side. Robert, there is no evidence of any frontal development whatsoever.

ROBERT Nature has not been exactly generous to Lesley.

GENERAL She, he or it has no bottom at all.

ROBERT She hasn't eaten for long stretches at a time.

GENERAL She has no hips.

ROBERT She has two of them, but they're on the narrow side. But I'll tell you what she has got. She's got the most lovely and fragile and bony feminine face.

GENERAL That I admit I haven't seen. God knows I want you to be happy, son. I only ask you these questions because I must know where I stand with you . . .

ROBERT Oh, why all this fuss about human relations? Can't we just agree we're independent of one another, and leave it at that?

GENERAL If that's the case, why did you come here at all?

ROBERT Mother implored me to. I gave in, more out of weakness than anything else.

GENERAL I see. There are certain facts of life, Bob, which must be accepted by both of us, whether we like it or not.

ROBERT I know them.

GENERAL I daresay you do, but I'm a methodical and repetitive old codger . . .

ROBERT Yes, you are.

GENERAL Yes, I am. And in spite of appearances, I may still be able to surprise you. You're my son, I'm your father.

ROBERT Oh!

GENERAL Even by ignoring our chance relationship, you are conscious of it. At worst it gives you something to work hard at forgetting. I have a different, and perhaps more constructive view of it than you. If I am of no service to you, I find it regrettable. You, however, have been of great service to me, and I wish to thank you for it.

ROBERT Aren't we being a little sentimental?

GENERAL I don't think so. I hope not. You are trying to goad me into an unnatural attitude·by attempting to be as odious as possible. It won't work, simply because I have far more stamina than you. I'm older. I've more to complain about and consequently, I complain a great deal less. I'm going to tell you something that'll surprise you. I understand your rebellion. I even approve of it.

ROBERT You're joking.

GENERAL No, I'm not. You have taken the law into your own hands. I never did. But you have rebelled half-heartedly—and I flatter myself I never did anything by halves. I accepted the world I was given, and I asked no questions. I chose a life of obedience, and I obeyed . . . often against my better judgment. But now, Bob, I've retired. And if there are any experiments with freedom to be done, by Jove, I'm game . . .

RORERT (*Worried*) What do you mean?
     (*The door bursts open, and there stands* JUDY, *a very pretty girl in a kind of maternity mini-skirt and colored stockings. She dashes over enthusiastically and embraces her father*)

JUDY Daddy!

GENERAL Judy! My darling little girl. Let me look at you! My, you've put on weight!

JUDY That's one way of putting it.(*She giggles; casually*) Robert.
(*He doesn't reply*)

ROBERT Now, what are you going to make of that?

GENERAL (*After a considerable pause. Gently*) Don't you think it might have been polite to have written and told me that you were engaged?

JUDY Engaged? I'm not engaged.

GENERAL (*Slowly*) Married then.

JUDY I'm not married either.

GENERAL (*Slowly*) Oh well, contemplating marriage then.

JUDY (*Lighting a small cigar*) I'm not contemplating marriage.

GENERAL (*Slowly*) Divorced then.

JUDY I'm not divorced.

GENERAL (*After a moment*) You're right, Robert . . . I'm too old. (*He pulls himself together and speaks to himself*) No, no, steady, Fitzbuttress . . . the world belongs

29

to the young, you've *got* to understand if you're going to survive . . . (*Aloud*) I presume . . . I presume that protuberance is not entirely due to a surfeit of cream buns.

JUDY (*Merry*) No. I'm pregnant.

GENERAL Pregnant! Of course you are! Jolly good! By the look of you, it should have arrived about two months ago.

JUDY Any time now.

GENERAL And you say there is no man involved.

JUDY There's no man I'd care to marry involved.

GENERAL You fell out with him.

JUDY I fell out with them.

GENERAL Oh, there's more than one father? Who are the blighters?

JUDY Frankly, I don't know which one it was.

GENERAL Oh well, in that case it's much wiser not to marry.

JUDY That's my point of view.

GENERAL Why are you so possessive? May I share your point of view?

JUDY Certainly. But you don't.

GENERAL   How can you be sure?

JUDY   You can't.

GENERAL   I can't? Why not?

JUDY   You're of another generation.

GENERAL   Yes, that's quite true. And so will your child be.
And what if your child agrees with me? That'll be just
his bad luck, won't it?

JUDY   By then we'll have a fully emancipated society.

ROBERT   Ha, ha.

GENERAL   However emancipated the society is, Judy, it is
possible to have unemancipated people in it. You can't
presume to know what your kid will be like. You can guess
what conditions will be like, but not what your child will
be like. I had no idea when I first saw Robert in the Gibral-
tar Military Hospital—a dear pink little bundle—I had
no idea that one day he'd look like a leftover from the Last
Supper, and would be living with a bass singer he must
have met in a mirror. I had no idea you'd come to me in a
skirt as long as a trouser cuff, exploding with a fatherless
child and smoking a cigar. I mean, these are things you
just can't foresee.

JUDY   What are you trying to prove, Dad?

GENERAL   I'm not trying to prove anything, Judy. I'm
merely suggesting that your offspring may be of a tempera-

ment to need a father more than he or she ever needs a mother. What then?

JUDY   These are hurdles we should take when we come to them, as you used to say.

GENERAL   I never referred to a father as a hurdle. You seriously think that, if your child desires a father, you can procure one for him, just like that?

JUDY   Oh Lord, yes.

ROBERT (*Agreeing wisely*)   Nowadays, yes.

GENERAL   You mean to tell me that there are men who are willing to become fathers first and husbands second?

JUDY and ROBERT   Oh yes. Nowadays. Yes.

GENERAL   Well, I'll take your word for it.

JUDY   There are plenty of men with wives who have left them, and who have custody of a young child or children of their own. Such men are only too eager to get married.

GENERAL   Oh, so your little nipper gets a little brother or sister in the bargain. A little brother or sister with which it has nothing in common.

ROBERT   Judy and I have nothing in common, however official your marriage was.

JUDY   You can say that again.

GENERAL   You have your parents in common.

JUDY   Not really. I only like you. Can't stick Mother. Robert dotes on her. Hates you.

GENERAL   Really. So, in fact, we're two families living under the same roof.

ROBERT   Linked by common furniture and fittings.
(*There is a deep sound*)

GENERAL   What's that?

ROBERT   It's Lesley. She is singing "The Death of Boris" to Mother.

GENERAL   But would . . .

ROBERT   Sshhh!

GENERAL   But would either of you contemplate a love match?

JUDY   I'd have an affair out of physical attraction, but I don't see the point of marriage. It only leads to divorce, doesn't it? And is that any better for the kids than no marriage? It's messy and dirty, and hypocritical.

GENERAL   There are a few marriages which don't end up in divorce court.

ROBERT   Can you honestly say your marriage is as passionate now as it was at the beginning?

33

GENERAL   No, of course not.

ROBERT   And can you honestly say that you're not sometimes tempted by a new experience?

GENERAL   Mother's not coming, is she? Of course I'm
tempted, but does temptation exist in this world to be re-
sisted or to be given in to?

RORERT   If it's given in to, as you say, it's no longer a temptation, is it?

GENERAL   I suppose not.

ROBERT   Temptation only comes with the second thought.
I'm never tempted. I just do what I feel like.

JUDY   I don't even have to agree with you. Look at me.

GENERAL   But doesn't it make you both very selfish?

JUDY   If everyone's selfish, it rather cancels itself out,
doesn't it?

ROBERT   Most of the trouble in this world is caused by those
who have other people's interests at heart. Look at the
world today. It's full of soldiers protecting freedom where
they're not wanted, and their presence stamps out the very
freedom they think they're protecting.

GENERAL   (With passion)   That's absolutely true. Full
marks.

ROBERT   And what has the Church done? Sent missionaries into the lightest corners of the globe to darken them with feelings of guilt and the inescapable nightmare of Original Sin. And while they were about it, they upset the delightful, instinctive sexual mores of those places. According to the Kinsey report, our usual manner of making love is called by the Polynesians, "The Missionary Position." Amen.

JUDY   Dad, don't you sometimes wish you'd dared to lead a fuller life?

GENERAL   Fuller? In what sense?

JUDY   That you'd dared to live instead of dream?

ROBERT   Judy means, don't you wish you'd had lots of affairs instead of being faithful?

GENERAL   No.

ROBERT   Isn't that just a conditioned reflex of your upbringing?

GENERAL   Yes. Yes, it probably is.

ROBERT   Then there must be opportunities you regret not having taken.

GENERAL   (*Smiling distantly. Nostalgically. Charmingly*) Yes. Yes, there are . . . (*Clearing his throat*) And yet I'm proud of my abstinence.

35

JUDY   Proud . . . but unsatisfied.

GENERAL   (*Puzzled*)   Unsatisfied? . . . I don't think so. We were never trained to expect very much, you know.

ROBERT   Then what's the point of living? Your generation was born old.

GENERAL   We were born the same age as everybody else, but brought up old. Puritanical, I suppose. It seems damn silly now—the fact that my parents paid huge sums of money to expensive schools so that I should sleep on a hard bed and wash in ice-cold water in midwinter and be underfed. (*Thoughtfully*) And yet, you know, Bob, it did me *some* good. It prepared me for life.

ROBERT   It prepared you for the life of your generation and your class—the war to end wars, polo in India, shooting it out with the frontier tribes, truce for tiffin—but there won't be any wars in our time. We just won't go. It's too stupid. It's a waste. Discipline, as you know it, has gone for a Burton. When I'm told to do something, my reaction is to ask why, not to jump to it.

GENERAL   Your chronology is a little confused, Robert. I missed the war to end wars. I was in time for the next one. Still, I am more than inclined to listen to you both with respect. A fellow doesn't like to lose touch, and so long as he's alive, he's in duty bound to understand what's going on around him. But explain to me—slowly, as to a backward pupil—what are the advantages of your way of thinking?

ROBERT   You tell him, Judy. I find this kind of argument exhausting.

GENERAL   I'm so sorry to have exhausted you.

JUDY   Oh Bob, you're frightfully rude.

GENERAL   I'm prepared to believe, Judy, that rudeness is part of an advanced philosophy of life which I am too hidebound to fully comprehend, but at least I am trying.

JUDY   Well, Dad, let's say you'd had many affairs.

GENERAL (*Patiently*)   Yes.

JUDY   You are an old man now. Right?

GENERAL   If you say so.

JUDY   Wouldn't those affairs have given you much more to look back on? I mean, I'm young, but already I can look back on some wonderful experiences and some pretty awful ones, and I reckon I'm richer for them—while you, at your advanced age, have a panorama of Mother at various ages to look back on, and that's all.

GENERAL (*Reasonably*)   Yes, I must say, that's a somewhat limiting retrospect. But is life entirely made up of physical contacts? Aren't there other things?

JUDY   Oh, yes, but I think the physical side of life is most important. I feel that the human body is a wonderful instrument—and it is up to me to play it to the full—to ex-

37

tract all the poetry and music from it. The mind can look after itself. (*Long pause. The* GENERAL *reflects.* JUDY *continues gently*) I know you must be feeling that you have failed in your responsibility. It's not true, Dad. You've been a wonderful father. (ROBERT *snorts*) You just can't compete with the swinging times we live in.

GENERAL (*Somberly, and equally gently*) If you must know, I wasn't thinking that at all. The idea of personal failure never entered my head. It never does. Not even when the Japs had us on the run with eighteen divisions against two and a half, and with the swollen Irrawaddy River behind us did the idea of personal failure even enter my head. I was far too frigging angry. No—I was silent for a moment just now because I thought to myself what a waste it is—here are young people with all the right ideas—negative, but right—of brushing aside the humbug we swallowed with our mother's milk. I give you full marks for thinking for yourselves, for finding rational arguments with which to implement your spontaneous emotions. And yet, in the final analysis, you just won't have the guts to see your dreams through to their logical conclusion.

JUDY (*Outraged*) I won't have the guts? Look at me!

GENERAL Anyone can get themselves into that condition— any woman, that is. The proof of the pudding . . . darling, I wish you wouldn't smoke those beastly cigars. The proof of the pudding will come when the child is born, and when you *can't* think exclusively of yourself. Then you'll come slap up against society at its worst, at its most stupid, at its most unforgiving. You'll put up a front for a time, pretending you don't care what people say, but as the child grows, and begins to think and even talk, you'll take refuge in conventional morality. You'll try and put his name down for one of the better schools, if they still exist, you'll invent a tragic past for yourself—"Daddy died in a car smash" or some such fiction. You won't have the guts to see it through.

JUDY (*Cold*) How d'you know?

GENERAL (*Thuderous*) Because I'm a leader of men, damn it. That's how I know! I can read character when I see it! (*Quieter*) As for Robert, he's chosen indolence—that's a safer wicket than yours, Judy—and there's nothing new about it or revolutionary. Naturally, such a life has its advantages. By disengaging you never risk defeat, and you never try for victory. You're as healthy and as sweet-smelling as stagnant water.

ROBERT (*Indolent*) That was the outburst I have been waiting for.

GENERAL No, it wasn't. You expected me to burst with righteous indignation when I found out you'd been sent down from Oxford. I didn't. You expected me to be horror-struck when I saw you in the company of a weird hermaphrodite. I wasn't. You expected me to react as the conventional Victorian father. Did I? On the contrary, I endorsed your criticism of society. I agreed with many of the points you had to make. I flattered your intelligence, I even found your appearance quite refreshing. All I said, and say again, is that you are not equipped to exploit your

39

opinions. It's a pity. It's a crying shame. It's totally inadequate.

(LADY FITZBUTTRESS *enters with* LESLEY)

LADY   Have you finished your tête-a-tête? Oh, Judy, I didn't hear you enter. Lesley has just given me a most enjoyable half hour of music.

GENERAL   No, she hasn't. We're all saying what we think from now on, Doris. It's the order of the day. Lesley could be heard from here, unfortunately. She has no musical talent whatsoever, and a perfectly beastly voice. (LESLEY *stamps petulantly*) Angry, Lesley? Good.

ROBERT (*Rising, cross*)   What do you hope to achieve by irritating Lesley?

GENERAL   Now, there's the outburst I have been waiting for. As conventional as they come. The reaction of the average General.

ROBERT (*Taking* LESLEY'*s hand*)   Lesley happens to be my mistress. I do have some loyalties.

GENERAL   I am absolutely thunderstruck to hear it.

ROBERT   Lesley and I can do without your sarcasm, can't we, my darling?

LESLEY (*In her deepest diapason*)   Yes.

ROBERT   Let's go out of here.

GENERAL   No need to. I'm leaving.

LADY   Tubby!

GENERAL   Oh, not in a huff, Doris. In friendship—and only temporarily. I'm going to the Hanover Arms Hotel for a while to think things over. You may not know it, but before any large-scale military operation, it was always my rule to isolate myself for a while from all my advisors, in order to enter into a personal state of grace in which I could see the problems of the day and my own duty with crystal clarity. Since I haven't unpacked, I have no need to waste time packing. I won't need a taxi. I'll walk into the village. If it's born in my absence, Judy, just send me a wire with the sex. Good luck to you all.

LADY   Please don't leave, Tubby.

GENERAL   No tears, now, Doris. It's been four years. It might as well be a couple of weeks longer.

JUDY   Daddy!

GENERAL   What?

JUDY   Don't go!

GENERAL   I'm free too, Judy. I want to go. I will go, believe me—but I'll be back once I've assimilated all the new thoughts you've crammed into this old man's head of mine. My regards to the neighbors, Doris, and—oh, I never kissed you on arrival. (*He kisses her*) Good-by, my dear. (*He turns at the door*) And *vive la liberté!*
     (*He exits*)
                    Curtain

Act Two

Anthony Quayle as GENERAL SIR MALLALIEU FITZBUTTRESS and Sam Waterston as ROBERT.

It is nighttime and the stage is dark. We are suddenly aware of a muffled noise, a giggle or two, an occasional note of rising passion. A light appears down the stairs. LADY FITZBUTTRESS *stands there, silhouetted in her nightdress. She has a sword in her hand.*

LADY   Who's in there? (*Silence*) I know you're in there, whoever you are, so you might as well come out. I warn you, I'm armed. (*Silence*) Oh, very well then.
    (*She switches on the light*)

ROBERT   (*His voice comes from the direction of the floor*) Turn out the light, Mother. We're naked!
    (LADY FITZBUTTRESS *gasps*)

LADY   What are you doing there, Robert?

ROBERT   That's a silly question if ever I heard one, Mother.

LADY   Well, I think it's utterly reprehensible.
    (*She switches off the light*)

ROBERT   I know you do.

LADY   I didn't even know you were here. You haven't been home for a month now, and when you do deign to drop in, instead of coming up to see me, you use the drawing room as a . . . as a . . . whatever the decent word for it is.

ROBERT I got here at five o'clock this morning, Mother. I thought it was politer to wait until breakfast rather than wake you up in the middle of the night.

LADY Whoever comes on a visit in the middle of the night? Couldn't you have waited until this morning to arrive, and indulge your passion for Lesley elsewhere?

ROBERT Where? On the railway embankment—and get arrested for indecent exposure? Why've you got Dad's sword in your hand?

LADY First of all, I thought you were a burglar—and I was not far wrong. Secondly, if I know Mallalieu, he'll be back today. It's his annual regimental reunion tonight, and he's never missed one if he's been in the country.

ROBERT Ra,ra,ra! You can put on the lights now, Mum. We're decent.
(*She does so.* ROBERT *sits up. With him is* HELGA)

LADY (*Amazed*) Helga! Where's Lesley?

ROBERT In the garden, I imagine.

LADY (*Irritated*) It's five forty-five in the morning. She can't always be in the garden. As for you, Helga . . . words fail me.

HELGA I'm sorry, madame. It was just the folly of the moment. I had a quarrel with my English teacher, and I felt so lonely.

46

LADY   You realize, of course, that I'm responsible for you toward your parents? I had to sign a document accepting responsibility for your safety while you are in my employment.

HELGA   Am I fired?

LADY   It may be too late to fire you, for all I know. You may have to stay as my daughter-in-law, which would be more than I could bear.

ROBERT   We were only petting.

LADY   What does that mean? I dread to think.

ROBERT   We were just horsing around.

LADY   Well, I'm not going to tell you again what I think about all this. You know perfectly well. And to think of poor Lesley in the garden. (*Abruptly*) But I didn't think you and Helga even knew each other.

ROBERT   We don't. It's much more exciting that way.

HELGA (*Mournful*)   I left my keys behind. I started throwing stones at the window, but you know me . . . I always miss. Instead of hitting your window, I hit the window next door.

ROBERT   I heard her, and came down and . . . let her in.

LADY   And then you made love on the floor.

47

ROBERT (*Imitating his father*)   Now you're in the pictchah!

LADY   That's a lie, all that. There's always a key under the mat, you know that, Helga. You saw a light in the guest room, and you were intrigued by it.

HELGA   Ja, there was an element of that, I admit it.

LADY   And as for you, Robert, why did you tell me that Lesley was in the garden? She's not here at all, is she? You've left her.

ROBERT   Lesley *is* here.

LADY   D'you swear it?

ROBERT   I swear it.

LADY   May I sit down?
(HELGA *moves close to* ROBERT)

ROBERT   Thank you, Mother.

LADY   Oh my God! What are we going to do now?

ROBERT   Wait, I suppose.

LADY   Wait for what?

ROBERT   Everything, as always. The dawn. The morrow. Dad's ceremony. The consequences.

LADY What consequences? (*A baby starts screaming upstairs. They all look up. Pause.*) Helga Rasmussen, I'm going to phone the agency in the morning. You can go back to Stavanger.

HELGA (*Gloomy*) If you send me away, I'll kill myself.

LADY (*Rising*) I'll confiscate your pills.

HELGA There are other ways. I'll jump out of the window.

LADY (*With rising hysteria*) I forbid you to go upstairs.

HELGA (*Dramatic*) Then I'll jump out of a downstairs window.

LADY (*Beside herself*) You deserve a good spanking!

HELGA Sadist!

LADY What? What are you accusing me of now?

ROBERT (*Dry*) A sadist, Mother, is a person who enjoys inflicting physical pain.

HELGA (*Philosophical*) Not only physical.

ROBERT Why don't you do it, Mum—with the flat side of Dad's sword? It's a marvelous erotic novelty.

LADY (*Tense*) It'd give me no pleasure whatever to inflict physical pain, but if I use the sword at all, it'll be the blade, believe me. What are you, some kind of satyr, or something? Where does it come from, this obscene preoccupation for what the senses can offer?

ROBERT (*Dreamy*) By God, you're an attractive bitch.

LADY Don't call me that!

ROBERT I was talking to Helga. I'm not Oedipus, Mother. I've never seen her in the light until now. Is that hair its natural color?

HELGA Yes. The eyes too.

LADY (*Shouting*) Helga! You will pack your bags at once!
(*The child renews its screaming*)

ROBERT There, you've wakened that child again, Mother. I wish it'd shut up.

LADY It's a perfectly lovely child! I hope it screams the place down. It saves me the trouble.

ROBERT (*Patient*) Why don't you go back to bed now, Mother? You know there are no burglars. You can sleep in peace.

LADY Sleep in peace? Helga, come upstairs at once and pack your bags. That is an order!
(*The effect is somewhat spoiled by* JUDY's *entrance. She is furious*)

JUDY (*Who is obviously no longer pregnant*)   How can I ever get that child to sleep with this infernal noise going on? Surely you ought to know better, Mother.

LADY   I should know better? I'm fed up with your impertinence, Judy! I am your mother, you know!

JUDY   That's the only reason I suggested you ought to know better.

LADY   That child? That child? Why do you always refer to it as *that child*? If Andrew is crying, it's probably because he's hungry.

JUDY (*Fuming*)   I have just breast-fed the little bastard!

LADY   Don't call him that!

JUDY   It's not derogatory, it's a fact. He drank about six gallons of milk, as far as I could make out.

LADY   Then he needs to be burped.

JUDY   He brought up about two hundred massive belches. Now he's about ready for by-bys, but obviously, with this bloody racket going on, he can't make his journey to the land of Nod.

ROBERT   The sandman is a little late today.

JUDY   Shut up, you. You're probably the cause of it all, knowing you.

LADY   I found him down here, making love to Helga.

JUDY   To Helga?

LADY   On the rug.

JUDY   It hardly matters where, Mother. Where's Lesley?

LADY   In the . . . somewhere . . .

JUDY   You take my advice, you two. Think of the consequences before you do anything silly.

HELGA   I love babies.

JUDY   Do you? You love the *idea* of babies.

HELGA   Something that depends on you . . . that grows inside you . . .

JUDY   Intensely lovely it all is. Natural, too. Natural. I thought so too—I was so bloody broad-minded, I walked around as though I were naked. What I didn't bargain for is that babies are so *damned selfish!* They scream just whenever they feel like it, and you become their slave for no other reason than that you're old enough to know better.

HELGA (*Horrified*)   But have you no maternal instincts?

JUDY   My maternal instincts lasted about two to three weeks.

ROBERT (*Pontifical*) Babies are free.

JUDY They're free, and what do they do with their freedom except cling to you and take away yours?

LADY (*Calmly and bitterly triumphant*) Yes, and wait till they grow old enough to answer back, and to think for themselves, and to reject you, and to sleep with the Scandinavian help . . . on your rug. Your troubles are only just beginning. (*With contained self-pity*) Mine, thank heaven, are almost over . . .
　　　(*They all become aware of a silence*)

JUDY (*Dramatic*) Why's he stopped crying? (*No reply is forthcoming*) Mother? He may have asphyxiated himself!
　　　(*She rushes out*)

LADY (*Quiet*) There. Judy at last is growing up. It always takes a little longer for a man.

ROBERT (*Starting*) What's that?

LADY What?

ROBERT A noise in the garden.

LADY (*Sighing*) It's probably Lesley.
　　　(*The* GENERAL *enters from the garden, crossing toward the stairs*)

GENERAL Good morning, Doris.

LADY (*Shocked*) Mallalieu! Mallalieu! What has happened?

GENERAL The regimental dinner's tonight. I came back for my medals and my sword . . . Oh, you've got it there. What are you doing with my sword, Doris?

LADY I thought I heard burglars.

GENERAL Burglars? Oh, and it was only me.

LADY It was Robert and Helga making love.

GENERAL I prefer her to Lesley any day. (*Takes the sword from* LADY FITZBUTTRESS) Here, Doris, give me that.

LADY That is not the point, Mallalieu.

ROBERT Dad. What are you doing dressed up like that?

GENERAL I'm the new recruit reporting for duty, Robert. Are my toenails long enough?

ROBERT Toenails!

GENERAL No, I don't think I'm fully qualified yet, but give me time.

LADY I've had your uniform pressed.

GENERAL Thank you, but I won't be needing it. I'll pin the medals to this.

ROBERT   You're not going like *that!*

GENERAL   Why not? It'll do them good to be jolted from their confounded complacency.

ROBERT (*Condescending*)   But you can't belong to two worlds at once, Dad.

GENERAL   I repeat—why not? There's nothing about it in regulations. I have a perfect right to wear my medals. I won them. They're mine. I also have a perfect right to wear civilian clothes. I've retired.

ROBERT   But . . . you're barefoot.

GENERAL   I'm not well enough known as yet in the circles in which you move to be able to borrow footwear at will.

LADY   But you had perfectly good shoes when you left here.

GENERAL (*Patient*)   What would I be doing with *perfectly good* shoes, Doris? Once my shoes were *perfectly good,* I preferred no shoes at all.

LADY   But . . . where have you been all this time?

GENERAL   All over the place. Last night it was Sunning Dale.

ROBERT   Sunning Dale? You must have left at midnight.

GENERAL   Well after midnight, Bob. It might take you six hours to get here from Sunning Dale, because you'd walk

—it took me precisely five hours and four minutes, because I marched.

LADY   You marched? You must be hungry, Mallalieu.

GENERAL   That's quite all right, Doris. I thought of that. I've got my own with me. I'll just set up my own bivouac over here.

LADY   Oh dear, let me get you some proper food.

GENERAL   No, no, I prefer my own hard tack. No offense, Doris.

LADY (*Overwhelmed*)   But what were you doing in Sunning Dale, Tubby? We don't know anyone there.

GENERAL   Exactly. I don't do my apprenticeship near people I know, Doris. I told you I would only make an appearance again once I felt I was ready.

ROBERT   It's hopeless, Dad. Now that you're here, I wish you'd just go upstairs and shave and be your normal self.

GENERAL (*Cold*)   That's what you want, isn't it? It justifies your behavior to feel that you're reacting against something, doesn't it? And it suits your ego to have a father with a clipped mustache, a red neck, and retrogressive ideas. Well, I'm not going to make it that easy for you.

LADY   I wish you'd do as Robert says, dear.

GENERAL   Robert has never done what I say. Why on earth should I start doing as he says?

ROBERT   Can't you see what he's up to, Mum? He's trying to shame me into going back into society.

LADY   Oh! In that case it's a very plucky attempt.

GENERAL   (*Smiling grimly*)   That may have been my original idea, Robert, admittedly—but I didn't reckon with one thing.

ROBERT   And what's that?

GENERAL   (*Cackling*)   I'm enjoying myself.

ROBERT   (*Sits up in real alarm*)   You're doing what?

GENERAL   I've never had a consistently better time in my life. It takes me back to the good old days learning field-craft . . . preparing man-traps, laying fires, following spoor, covering tracks . . . and I've started listening to the night again . . . have you ever done that, Robert? . . . The miraculous sound of silence, in which every crackle of a twig sounds like a Howitzer . . . and the smell of the earth at night—it's entirely different, you know . . . a warm, sweet smell of tremendous intensity . . . a marvelous, rich, generous exhalation of a force so huge that you're no more than a microbe resting on its outer crust.

ROBERT   (*A howl*)   But Dad, you've got it all wrong. You've become a tramp, not a hippie!

GENERAL   (*With dignity*)   As I see it, the tramp is to the hippie what the working man is to the idle rich. The tramp works hard at not working; the hippie is content to just do nothing. Take your guitar, for instance. You don't know one end of it from the other.

ROBERT (*Hotly*) What about you?

GENERAL What about me? (*Strums his guitar*) Me? Aha! I acquired this instrument with a handbook—Play the Guitar Like Segovia in Twenty Lessons—it's really quite ingenious, a system of numbers. I've given myself thirty-two lessons so far, and I can pick out the tone of the regimental march and most of "God Save the Queen" with only a few minor errors in harmony. Look here. One— eighteen—twelve—twenty-four—some speak of Alex— oh, drat Alex-ander, and some—sixteen, sixteen, where's sixteen?—And some of He-e-e-rcules, some speak of— nine, nine—ah, there you are—and such a brave me-e-en as these. Can you do that?

ROBERT I don't *want* to do that!

GENERAL Exactly. Haven't the staying power.

LADY What an extraordinary idea! Never, in a month of Sundays, did I imagine you buying a guitar.

GENERAL I *earned* the guitar, selling matches.

ROBERT But you bought the matches.

GENERAL Well, obviously I had to start somewhere. You can't become a full-scale hippie these days on no capital whatever!

LADY (*Sighing*)   Well, it's been a jolly good joke.

GENERAL   Joke? Look here, if I'm going to be at the Horse Guards by this evening, I'd better set out now. I don't think I could face another forced march. I'll just go upstairs to pin on the medals.

ROBERT   Dad, you smell.

GENERAL   How on earth can you tell?

LADY   It's true, Mal . . . you are quite unsavory.

GENERAL   What you smell on me is earth, not dust—horse manure, not the effluvia of psychedelic coffeehouses.

LADY   I'm sure you're right, Mal, you usually are. But I don't care for the smell and I don't think the regiment will either. After all it's not a cavalry regiment, you know.
        (JUDY *enters*)

JUDY   Dad! I thought I heard your voice . . . (*She steps back*)

GENERAL   Don't be silly. You've had your own pony. Oh, by the way—congratulations.

JUDY   Thanks.

GENERAL   Thank you for the telegram. Found me in a ditch outside of Shrewsbury. So it's a boy!

JUDY Yes, it's a very noisy, overweight boy who doesn't even look a bit like me.

GENERAL You think there are doubts about its maternity as well?

JUDY No, alas. No.

GENERAL More than you bargained for?

JUDY (*Guardedly*) No.

GENERAL (*Rueful*) Not yet, eh? Can I see it?

JUDY No, you're far too dirty. I mean, what is the point of sterilizing bottles and washing everything in boiling water? . . . What are you up to, Dad. Have you escaped from somewhere?

LADY (*Genteel*) Your father has found happiness, Judy.

JUDY Oh, don't be ridiculous, Daddy! Whom are you trying to impress? Robert? Happiness, did you say?

LADY (*With icy sweetness*) Happiness is what he said.

GENERAL What's so shameful about happiness, Doris? Are you annoyed because I'm really and truly happy instead of just pretending to be, Doris? (*Gentle*) Happiness was written all over our faces as we tricked the neighborhood into thinking all was right with us—and the others undoubtedly did the same to us. For some reason people think they have won a victory if they successfully disguise their domestic disenchantment, but they never bother to make the same effort for the sake of their children as they do for total strangers. Children are regarded as part of the family, and therefore deserving victims of all that is sordid in human relationships.

LADY (*Shocked*) Mallalieu!

GENERAL Oh yes, we have had our rows, telling ourselves that the children were asleep, or too young to understand. We used to leave the door ajar so we could hear them, never imagining they could hear us. So they have grown up seeing through us at least as clearly as we see through one another. What have they learned from us but a keen sense of disgust and an instinctive loathing for hypocrisy?

LADY Tubby! I think you owe us an apology.

GENERAL Oh, Doris! I apologize readily to whoever is willing to accept it. You, the children, the Government, the Malayan bandits—I apologize for everything I may or may not do tomorrow and the day after. But that's not the point. The point is that the revolt of our children is entirely justified. I approve of it, d'you understand? All I regret is that they haven't the experience or the sheer moral fiber to see it through.

ROBERT That's ridiculous!

HELGA No it isn't. I understand.

LADY Kindly leave the room, Helga. This is a family row.

HELGA You said yourself I may already be part of the family. I agree with the General. My generation is confused

and bitter without knowing why. We give our bodies just
because we have been told by our parents that it is our most
precious possession. But how can we trust what they have
taught us, because those who taught us brought no happiness to themselves with their teachings. But we're not evil,
you know. We just don't know much about love, because
so much that is false is written about it and said about it
that it doesn't correspond with what we know and what
we see. And when we give our bodies it is often out of pity,
or friendship, or in a bad moment, out of curiosity—but
we don't feel that we are sinning, because we have seen
what is right bring much misery and often what is wrong,
bring much happiness. I understand you, General—because I am a country girl—and where I come from, there
are so many rivers and mountains to be lonely in, but
somehow one is never alone. The town seems empty compared to the countryside. If only we had any sense, we
would perhaps find the truth in those places we take for
granted . . . places which are so close to us, we have
forgotten to explore them.

GENERAL That's very eloquent, Helga . . . but what
exactly are you leading up to?

HELGA (*Emotional*) You are a great man, a father to your
regiment, a leader, a man born to command—and yet
when you return home, nobody listens to you—they eat
your bread, drink your wine, and insult you. So you leave
again to challenge an even greater world—alone! It's not
fair!

GENERAL What's unfair about it?

62

HELGA   No man should be alone to face the huge horizons you have chosen. General, if you wish, I will come with you and share the nights with you.
   (*She stands*)

LADY (*Strident*)   I saw it coming. Don't encourage her, Mallalieu!

HELGA (*Emotional*)   Well?

GENERAL (*Chuckling softly, but curiously disturbed*)   It only goes to show. For years I've been covering myself with deodorants and after-shave lotions, and nobody has ever looked at me, except for Doris, of course. Now I let myself go, voluntarily, and the first thing you know, a damned attractive girl . . . (*He looks at her properly for the first time*) *damned* attractive . . . *damned* attractive . . .

LADY (*Tenuous*)   No!

GENERAL   Yes, Doris . . . volunteers for the wretched job of sharing my asphalt with me. I'd be lying if I said I wasn't tempted, Helga.

ROBERT (*Outraged*)   Dad, you couldn't! Not you! Why she's just a—I mean, she'd sleep with just anyone.
   (HELGA *slaps* ROBERT *resoundingly on the face*)

LADY   How dare you . . .

HELGA (*Furious*)   Now I understand why you wear your hair that long. It doesn't hurt so much when you get your face slapped!

63

GENERAL   We seem to have succeeded in making Robert jealous. Didn't know he had it in him. Full marks, young lady. I must say I'm more tempted now than before. It's all right. Don't worry, Robert. But all the same—no thank you. Doris, why are you looking so unhappy? (*Softly*) Don't you realize that what these young people are really lacking is a cause. It was so easy for us, "For King and Country," "God Is Love," "The only good German is a dead German," there were no end of them—and with each one came an often unworthy simplification called duty, which covered a multitude of sins by silencing a multitude of virtues. What have they got? The dissolution of Empire is hardly compatible with "For King and Country," Hiroshima is hardly compatible with God as the image of love, while "The only good German is a dead German" is hardly compatible with the fact that some friendly German tanks are at this moment holding summer exercises not twenty miles from here as our guests, in order eventually to protect us from God and the President of the United States only know who. It's a mess these children have inherited, and so what can they do but rub their parents' noses in it? Why are you crying, Helga?

HELGA   You have made me feel very young—and I'm no longer used to it.

GENERAL   Well, you taught me how to make you feel young by your own old words. Knowing what I do about you, how could I possibly take advantage of you? No, no. I'm no cause, Helga. I'm still finding my way among the hedgerows and the railway bridges. What's the time?

ROBERT (*Glum*) It's light out.

GENERAL I'm off then. What room is young . . . the child in?

JUDY Andrew. D'you want to see him?

GENERAL No, no. I don't want you to run any risk, but I wouldn't mind seeing a photo of him some day.

JUDY You can go in. He's asleep.

GENERAL No, Judy—I just wanted to know which room to avoid. I'll get my medals and I'll be off. I'd rather see him awake in any case.
     (GENERAL *exits. The baby begins screaming again*)

JUDY (*At her wits' end*) Oh!
     (*She goes out*)

LADY Helga . . . can I borrow some of your pills?

HELGA (*Hard*) No.

LADY (*Quiet*) You're a vicious, immoral little bitch, and I intend to tell your mother so.

HELGA She's quite likely to believe you. She's very much like you in many respects.

LADY That's all I need to hear. Well, of course, we have the same problems—except that I'm stuck with hers as well as mine. (*She looks at* ROBERT) Oh Robert, I'm miserable.

ROBERT   Yes, I imagine you are, Mother!

LADY   Is that all you can say?

HELGA   Oh leave him a little time to get over the shock, madame. He had it much worse than you.

LADY   Helga, it is not possible for a human being to absorb more punishment than I have in the past month. If you weren't such a little horror, I'd show you the family album, and there you'd see a picture of stability and decency. Robert in his bathtub . .

ROBERT   Mother, don't!

LADY   Silly, foolish, childish memories perhaps, and yet kindly and warm. The General shooting, myself at the hunt, Judy coming out. Oh dear, I'm going to cry. What has happened to it all now?

HELGA   The General explained it all to you.

LADY   I never understood his explanations. Never, from our wedding day, have I understood his explanations. He tried to explain to me how he beat the Japanese, but to this day, for the life of me, I can't understand why the Japanese didn't win.

HELGA (Livid)   It was your duty to understand, even if you didn't. That's what he expected from you—and what you failed to give him.

ROBERT   You're the most conventional of the lot of them!

HELGA   What if I am? Perhaps all of us are just waiting for the right opportunity to be conventional—that is possible. But what a dream to be conventional with an unconventional man!

ROBERT   That's absurd.

HELGA   Absurd? (*Calmly*) You say that because you're in shock. All you have is an image—and your father's taken that away from you. Now you're left with nothing but your mother in tears, and all your long hair won't help you there. You weren't born looking like you do now, you know. You were born like that dear little naked thing upstairs, with all your messy necessities and undignified habits.

LADY   Robert was never like that.

ROBERT   Shut up, Mummy!

LADY   Robert was different, although I say it myself. He only very rarely cried, and that's only when the pressure on his poor tummy was unbearable.

ROBERT   Mother, it's embarrassing. Can't you see that?

HELGA   Who's conventional now? Do you really need the illusion that you were different from others even when you were sitting on your chamber pot?

LADY   (*Triumphant*) He *was* different, that's what you won't understand. He had the dearest little way of calling out, "Ready, Mummy."

67

ROBERT   Oh no! For heaven's sake, shut up, Mummy!

LADY (*Shocked. Then quickly recovering, cold*)   And now he's changed. He's grown up. (*She cries bitterly*) Oh, it's too unfair. I take refuge in vagueness . . . in absent-mindedness! Change the subject. I'm not a bit absent-minded really . . . I just can't look life in the face any more.

> (ROBERT *stands there miserably, like a wet spaniel.* HELGA *looks at him mercilessly*)

ROBERT   What d'you expect me to do? It's not *my* fault, is it? It's Dad.

HELGA   What do I expect you to do? The conventional thing you're dying to do. Comfort your mother.

ROBERT (*Sotto voce*)   She's so stupid.

HELGA (*Sotto voce*)   It's too late to change that.

LADY (*Violent*)   I am *not* stupid!

ROBERT   I'm sorry, Mummy, I didn't mean you to overhear that. Cheer up. It's me. It's Robert.

LADY (*Grabbing his hand. Her eyes shut*)   Let me hold your hand . . . Robert . . . my son . . . let your poor old stupid mother gather what crumbs of comfort she can.

ROBERT   You're not stupid, dear . . . Just not terribly . . . I mean . . . just *not*.

68

John Tillinger as BASIL UTTERWOOD, Margaret Linn as JUDY, Graham Jarvis as the VICAR (*standing*), Eileen Herlie as LADY FITZBUTTRESS, Hanne Bork as HELGA, and Sam Waterston as ROBERT.

LADY We can't all be, can we? It's not great intelligence which makes the world go round . . . it's the human heart . . . the stupid human heart . . . we're all so interdependent, my darling . . . tell me if that's the wrong word . . . we need each other . . . Every time I see you, I remember the pain of your birth—no, don't struggle, Bob—my Bob . . . I was far too small to have you, you know that . . . but I refused any surgery . . . I wanted to have you the way nature intended . . .

ROBERT (*Struggling*) You've told me all this before. There's no need to repeat it.

LADY You know how much you weighed at birth?

ROBERT Yes, I do. Eleven pounds and four ounces.

LADY Eleven pounds and five and a half ounces!

ROBERT It goes up an ounce or two every time you tell it. I suppose it's natural. The story's growing up.

LADY (*Holding him in a grip of iron*) You can laugh, Robert . . . You get that from your father . . . your urbanity, your wit, your charm . . . I have none of that. I'm too honest, thank you very much. But you're my boy all the same . . . look me in the eye.

ROBERT I can see you, Mother, even if you can't see me.

LADY I love you, Robert, more than I've ever loved anything. Don't tell Judy. But if it hadn't been for you, I'd have been dead long ago.

HELGA (*Matter-of-fact*) Yes, well, I think I'll make breakfast this morning.

LADY You can't.

HELGA I can try.
(*Before she can leave, the* GENERAL *enters. He wears
his medals and his sword on his old clothes*)

GENERAL Ah, there you are. I'm off.

LADY Yes, yes, leave us.

GENERAL He's a funny-looking little fellow, Andrew.
Looks like me after a shower. Judy let me hold him. Took
to me at once, just like Helga did. There's a lot to be said
for dirt. Stopped crying as soon as he saw me, and started
playing with the mud in my beard. (*The baby cries
again*) There. He wants his dirty old granddad. Well, I'm
off to do battle with the Philistines, Bob. I may not have
lifted a finger in Malaya, but thanks to you I'm more than
making up for it now.

HELGA General. Don't forget us.

GENERAL I won't. Good-by.
(*He exits*)

ROBERT (*Struggling*) You can't just let him go like that.
He'll make a fool of himself.

LADY (*Vindictive*) Let him!

ROBERT   But it's not like him, a man in his position. If he makes a fool of himself, he'll make a fool of us, can't you see that?

LADY   You're right. Run after him, Robert. Stop him at any cost! (ROBERT *runs off, but stops at the door*) What's the matter?

ROBERT   I've got a stitch. It must have been that quick movement.

HELGA   You'll never catch him in any case.

ROBERT   It's not only that. Lesley may really be in the garden. I'm not joking. I can't face her at the moment.

LADY   Call the police then. Say he's had a nervous breakdown. Say something. Anything.

HELGA   I won't let you near the phone!

LADY   You won't what?

HELGA   Let him live his dream. He deserves it. (*She pulls the phone cord out of its socket*) Now I'll go and make breakfast.
   (*She exits*)

LADY   (*Melodramatic*)   Robert!

ROBERT   I think I'll go and help her . . .
   (*He goes*)

LADY (*Heartbroken*) Robert . . . (*There is an insistent tap at the window*) Who's that? Is it you back, Mallalieu? (*She shades her eyes*) Lesley, is it you? (*She undoes the window. An improbable-looking man forces his way in —stout, rubicund, with an aggressive mustache and choleric complexion. He wears a flat country cap and a relaxed check suit*) Tiny!

TINY Ssh!

LADY I told you never to come here during the daytime, Tiny.

TINY I had to. He's just left, hasn't he, dressed like a confounded scarecrow? I saw him march down the drive with a shouldered banjo singing "The British Grenadiers." A perfect disgrace.

LADY It's a guitar.

TINY It's a perfect disgrace. (*Powerfully*) Oh Doris, for how long are we going to allow this mockery to continue?

LADY Tiny! Tiny, please. Give me a little more time.

TINY I've given you twenty-six years already, Doris. That's over a quarter of a century. Surely that's sufficient for you to know your own mind?

LADY That was the war, dear. Mallalieu was away. I couldn't do anything while he was away.

TINY   It seems to me the very moment to do something . . . however, I was away too at that time, defending my country.

LADY   Give Mallalieu his due, Tiny. He was defending his country too, you know.

TINY (*Tetchy*)   I know. We were in the same regiment, remember?

LADY (*Radiant*)   Of course I remember. It enabled me to wear the regimental badge in diamonds in your honor, dear heart, without for a moment feeling unfaithful.

TINY (*Thickly*)   Oh God, I want you so badly, Doris.

LADY   Still?

TINY   Forever . . . forever . . .

LADY   You really must go now.

TINY   Let me take my cap off.

LADY   Oh look out! Aren't you going to the regimental re-union?

TINY   Naturally. Wouldn't miss it for the world. I'm driving up after lunch.

LADY   You'll see Mallalieu there.

TINY   What? Eh? He's not going there like that—dressed like that, I mean—the way I saw him on the drive?

73

LADY Yes, I'm afraid so.

TINY The fellow's around the bend . . . mad . . . he's gone too far at last.

LADY (*Suffering*) I know. I know. What can we do about it?

TINY (*With passion*) Make the break. Compel Mallalieu to face the consequences of his own folly.

LADY He wasn't always like this, you know.

TINY Every man carries the seeds of his eventual destiny within him, Doris. Mallalieu was always fated to lose his mind. I was always fated to love you and to comfort you and to give you what only I can offer.

LADY (*Nervous*) Tiny, I heard footsteps.

TINY (*Reckless*) Let them come, a whole army of footsteps. (*Urgent*) For God's sake, it isn't only your problem, Doris. It's Daisy. She's entirely let herself go since Paul was taken to prison. Drinking heavily, you know. I never know what's going to happen next. I simply can't stand the uncertainty. I mean, I'm a man with a hell of a lot to give, and it's all being wasted—going to seed—can't you see that?

LADY Of course I can, my darling.

TINY Then . . .

LADY (*Almost a whimper*) Not yet. Not quite yet . . .

74

TINY (*After a pause*)   You're asking me to go on as we have for the last twenty-six years . . . a few chance meetings a month.

LADY (*Coy*)   The occasional indiscretion.

TINY (*With intolerable bravery*)   Very well, Doris. It's better than nothing. I don't mind. Mark you, you know my attitude toward unfaithfulness and immorality—I won't have it near me—as a churchgoing Christian, it's anathema to me—but this is different—everything around us is tarnished, ugly, soiled—whereas, we're clean, you and I, dearest Doris.

LADY (*Fingering his hair*)   Were we always so pure, Tiny? Torquay?

TINY (*An echo of romance*)   Torquay . . . Cairo?

LADY (*Sighing*)   Cairo . . . Valetta, the Crown Royal Hotel?

TINY (*With relish*)   Valetta . . . (*Darkly*) Aldershot . . .
      (*They both look down in shame, troubled*)

LADY   Aldershot . . .

TINY   No, frankly, we were sinners then—but I never thought then we'd have to wait another fifteen years . . . (*Brightly and doggedly*) Still, I don't regret a moment of it. It was too damned beautiful—and I am convinced in my own mind and heart, Doris, that Our Lord forgives sins of sufficient beauty.

75

LADY (*In the grip of a sudden folly*) Kiss me, Tiny. (*They do kiss, hand to shoulder; abruptly*) I really do hear footsteps now—and the wheels of the breakfast trolley.

TINY It won't be long now, I swear it.
(*He rushes to the window*)

LADY Tiny, I think you would be happier going out the door.
(*He exits through the garden door. The door opens.*
ROBERT *enters from the kitchen*)

ROBERT Who was that, Mother?

LADY Who was what?

ROBERT There's been someone in here, hasn't there? Look, the window's open.

LADY It was Lesley. She's very upset. Oh, Robert, you ought to be ashamed of yourself.

ROBERT I'm afraid Helga's burned the toast.

LADY Did you hear what I said?

ROBERT Yes. I'm sorry I called you stupid before, Mother. I didn't mean to upset you.

LADY Oh, how nice of you to care.

ROBERT I care about a great deal—I can't always show how much I care.

LADY I don't understand.

ROBERT Perhaps that's why I tell you. Poor old Dad. His sense of responsibility's like an incurable disease. He'll never learn to be really selfish, that's his trouble. He'll keep popping back here to see what's going on. It'd serve him damn well right if I joined the Army.

LADY Oh, Robert, whatever you do, don't do that! It's become frightfully dangerous, especially in wartime. And then I hear that they select the officers on the basis of merit these days, so that you might find yourself sitting next to almost anybody in the mess. And they tell me, even Cairo—dear, old Cairo—is full of Egyptians.

ROBERT You can't think I meant that seriously, Mother. I said that as a joke.

LADY (*Realizing the joke, she laughs, then she hears the baby crying upstairs*) Really, Judy'll have to find herself a husband soon. She simply can't cope alone.

ROBERT I don't think anyone can, really.
        (*He goes to the window and follows foottracks across the rug toward* LADY FITZBUTTRESS)

LADY (*Nervously*) What are you doing, Robert?

ROBERT Lesley's feet seem to have shrunk in the rain— tiny, little muddy footsteps . . . (*The tracks lead directly to behind* LADY FITZBUTTRESS *on the couch.* ROBERT

stops there and sits next to her) Perhaps there was a
burglar after all? A tiny, little muddy burglar?
(LADY FITZBUTTRESS *looks away nervously*)
Curtain

Act Three

A bright morning, six months later. The French windows are open and the sunlight streams in. LADY FITZBUTTRESS *is in her finest garden-party paraphernalia, all fluff and flutter and flowers. She is in a very good mood. Also onstage is* JUDY, *in a similar kind of dress, and a young man of striking insignificance,* BASIL UTTERWOOD. *He wears glasses and his hair grows in little waves.*

LADY   It's a lovely day for a wedding.

BASIL   Yes.

LADY   What did you say, Basil?

BASIL   I said yes. I'm inclined to agree with you.

LADY   (*Sighing*)   It's so rare that there's any agreement in this house. (*She looks out the window*) There's only one shadow on my happiness now.
(*There is a noise of hammering*)

JUDY   He'll get over it. I bet he'll even come down for the wedding.

LADY   Why he wants to live in a tree, I simply cannot imagine.

JUDY   Be thankful he's off the road and off the front page.

LADY   Sometimes I feel sure I can see two figures up there.

JUDY   You can't tell among the leaves. He's doing the work of two men up there, that's what it is.

LADY   Perhaps.

BASIL   Em . . . there's just one question I feel I simply must ask—and I prefer to ask it in front of Lady Fitz-buttress.

LADY   Yes, Basil?

BASIL   Well, it's just that . . . marriage is a pretty important step in a person's life, man or woman.

LADY   Basil, it is *the* most important step.

BASIL   I'm glad you confirm my impression. You have much more experience than I have. But then since it's such an important step, shouldn't one go into it with one's eyes wide open?

LADY (*After a moment*)   That depends, my dear. Since love is blind, how can one's eyes be wide open?
   (*She laughs*)

BASIL   That's very true, I'm sure, since your observation must be the result of your experience, but I really haven't had time to fall in love very deeply.

LADY   You never know how deeply you are in love until you are married.

BASIL   Is that so? But there must be exceptions to that rule?

LADY   Are you suggesting that you are one?

BASIL   No, please don't misunderstand me. I am very fond of Judy. As fond as one can be of someone one has known for only a few hours, and most of that time in very inferior visibility.

LADY   What are you talking about? Did you meet in a fog?

BASIL   No. The fact is, I don't drink. At all, you understand, except for an occasional sherry at some festive occasion, or a half-glass of cider at a pinch—but I did on the evening I met Judy.

LADY   You were drunk?

JUDY   He wasn't at all. He'd just come in third in the mile at the White City, and he'd been made the reserve miler on the Olympic team. We were celebrating at Joe Taverners' flat, and Basil was absolutely sparkling, shimmering with wit and charm. I fell for him there and then.

BASIL   (*Horrified*)   You did? I don't remember a thing.

JUDY   (*Tenderly*)   It was a bewitching night.

BASIL   I'm glad someone enjoyed it. The next thing I know is a few days ago when Judy tracks me down at the White City, and stands there outside the change-rooms with a child in her arms, and tells me it's mine. Well, I mean, it's a small wonder I couldn't even manage a five-minute mile that day.

LADY   You should have been overjoyed!

BASIL   Yes, but the child doesn't even look like me.

LADY   It looks exactly like you.

BASIL   But both Judy and I are fairly dark. The child is blonde.

LADY   The color of a child's hair always changes. Judy was bald at birth. Who could have guessed that a crop of chestnut hair would sprout on her head one day?

BASIL   Yes, but Judy and I both have blue eyes. The child has brown eyes.

JUDY   My eyes go very dark when I'm wearing dark clothes.

BASIL   The child's dressed in white. His eyes are still brown.

JUDY (*Tender*)   Basil, whatever a woman may say, she *always* knows who the father of her child is. *Always.*

LADY   Yes, always.

JUDY   I'm not a promiscuous person. It could have been no one but you.

BASIL   You're willing to swear to that, are you?

LADY (*Stern*) Basil, marriage is built on trust. If you are going to start doubting Judy's word at this juncture, then I will seriously think twice about allowing her to go through with this wedding.

JUDY Oh, Mother!

LADY I mean it, Judy.

BASIL I didn't doubt her word—a couple is supposed to be of help to one another. I need her help, that's all. I need her help to see clearly where I'm going.

LADY Basil, do you trust Judy?

BASIL Well . . .

LADY Do you trust me?

BASIL Of course.

LADY Well, I trust her. Does that help you at all?

BASIL Yes. Yes, I think it does.

LADY Very well, then, that's that. (HELGA *enters in a wedding dress. She is slightly pregnant*) Helga. You look ravishing, my dear, all in virginal white! It suits your complexion, if nothing else.

HELGA (*Patting her stomach*) It doesn't show too much, does it?

JUDY Not too much. Just enough to make people wonder.

HELGA Judy, you are always so sweet.

LADY You've met Helga, haven't you, Basil? She is my son Robert's bride-to-be—who will be sharing the double wedding with you.

BASIL (*Smiles sheepishly*) Yes, we have met. When I arrived early this morning, it was Helga who opened the front door and showed me to my room. (LADY FITZBUT-TRESS *looks at* HELGA, *who crosses to the window*) I didn't realize this was to be a kind of mass wedding.

LADY You don't mind sharing, do you?

BASIL No, no. The more the merrier. I'm used to working with a team—it doesn't seem so bad, taking the plunge, if there's more than one of you.

LADY I don't much care for this idea of taking the plunge . . . (ROBERT *enters down the stairs*) Today is a joyous occasion for everyone.

HELGA He waved at me.

BASIL Basil Utterwood.
(*They shake hands*)

ROBERT Robert Fitzbuttress.

LADY Robert, let me look at you. (ROBERT, *laughing, crosses to* HELGA, *who is also convulsed*) Go out and show yourself to Daddy. (ROBERT *and* HELGA *are hugging*) No, no,

Helga, there's plenty of time for that . . . Go and let your father see you.

ROBERT   Oh, for God's sake. (*The* VICAR *is heard ringing his bike bell*) Oh, that'll be the Vicar. Vicar! Come in. The door's open.

LADY (*To all*)   It's the Vicar. He wanted to come by on his way to the church and investigate what he called "the lie of the land."
      (*The* VICAR *enters*)

VICAR   Good morning to you all, and a very good morning it is, too, Lady Fitzbuttress—quite fitting for nuptials.

LADY   Ah, this is Mr. Utterwood, Vicar—Judy's husband—well, almost.

VICAR   I have often admired you on the television, Mr. Utterwood, but as I only have a very small screen, and as you run so rapidly, you're never on it for very long.
      (*All laugh*)

BASIL (*Flattered*)   Oh . . .

LADY   And perhaps you remember Helga—who used to be the au-pair girl from far-away Norway.

VICAR   Oh, yes indeed—and quite a change seems to have come over you, too, my dear. When you first came here, you were a mere slip of a girl, but now you're a fine, strapping lass, aren't you? It's all that delicious creamery butter from the home farm. (*He laughs a little*) Well, Robert, it's quite a romance, isn't it? The prodigal returns and falls in love with . . .

ROBERT   The fatted calf.
     (*He and* HELGA *laugh and fall into an embrace*)

VICAR   Now, now. That is very definitely *not* what I intended to say—but it's all good fun—words are wonderful implements, aren't they, with which to fashion thoughts, and messages, and innocent repartee. Yes, Judy? How's young Andrew?

JUDY (*Without enthusiasm*)   Very well.

LADY   Very well, thank you, Vicar.

JUDY   Very well, thank you, Vicar.

VICAR (*Suddenly serious. He has the changes of mood of one who is accustomed to carrying on conversations on his own terms*)   Now, sit down everybody. (*They all obey and sit on the couch*) I very much wanted to have a chat with you all before the ceremony in order to satisfy my own mind that the nature of the great adventure—I like to refer to it as a great adventure—upon which most of you are embarking today is clearly understood by you all. Now I am sure I do not have to acquaint you with the delights of physical harmony . . . but I may be able to tell you a little about how those delights can be improved upon by assiduous rationing and what I like to call a sense of self-denial. Or let me put it another way. Christmas pudding

88

. . . would hardly be so delectable for one day of the year if it were a staple food like porridge, eaten all the year round. Sex should be considered as Christmas pudding rather than as porridge, the appetite for it sharpened by what? (*Pointing at* BASIL, *who doesn't answer*) Correct. Self-denial. Do you all follow me?

ALL (*Dutifully, in chorus*) Yes . . . mm . . .

VICAR (*Deadly earnest*) Good. Good. Now, Judy, you have made some pretty foolish mistakes, haven't you?

JUDY Yes, I have . . .

LADY Vicar . . .

JUDY Vicar.

VICAR (*With a bleak smile*) I am glad to hear you admit it. It is not my intention to induce you to shout "*Mea culpa*," or to cover yourself with sackcloth and ashes. No, no, those days are over—we too have learned to live with the times. I just want you to look the hard facts coldly and unemotionally in the face and to say to yourself, "I have been a fool, but now I have come together with God in the solemn act of holy wedlock"—wedlock—it's a good word, Judy—for to that lock you are today throwing away the key forever. (*He puts his hand on* JUDY's *shoulder; she jumps with surprise*) "And I will live the rest of my life in sanctity and the glow of a great love." Is that clear?

ALL Yes . . .

VICAR Splendid. Basil Utterwood, I know very little about you apart from your enviable reputation as a miler, but you, too, have known thoughtless temptation. You negligently sired an innocent child, but then our Lord spoke to you through the agency of the human conscience, and in a flash, you realized the callousness of your act, and came forward to give that child and its poor mother the full measure of your responsibility. Now you are to be a husband and a father at one and the same moment, a moral burden happily denied the majority of men. I hope you are ready for this herculean task?

BASIL (*Rises*) Not quite, no.
    (*There is a stir of alarm from* JUDY *and* LADY FITZ-BUTTRESS)

VICAR (*With bleak satisfaction*) Ah!

BASIL You said, sir, that I had negligently sired an innocent child. I am not usually negligent—a runner can't afford to be.

VICAR Quite.

BASIL But I must have been more than negligent on this occasion, because for the life of me I can't remember having done so.

VICAR (*Staggered*) You can't remember having indulged in the carnal act?

BASIL Absolutely not—so that I can't have really known thoughtless temptation either, can I? My mind was, frankly, on the Olympics at the time.

LADY Now, Basil, dear, I think we have agreed that you weren't quite yourself.

BASIL I had a glass or two of stuff described as "cup."

VICAR You mean alcohol was to blame?

BASIL It was cup. I thought it was nonalcoholic.

VICAR You are now saying you committed the sin of fornication while under the influence of a soft drink? (*He clears his throat*) We are treading on dangerous ground here. Let us face the facts. Your marriage has been arranged for eleven o'clock. Do you feel yourself ready for it?

BASIL You may not know this about me, sir, but I'm a Scoutmaster . . .

VICAR (*Giving the sign*) Oh, good show!

BASIL Yes, I saw your badge—and I take the Boy Scout movement very seriously. Our motto is, as you know . . .

VICAR and BASIL Be prepared.

BASIL (*Continuing*) I'm always ready for anything, sir. I have Lady Fitzbuttress' word that I am responsible, and so I'll go through with it, but if I am put on my Scout's oath, I'd have to reaffirm that I do not *feel* responsible. But I'll say this to you, Judy. Any Christian must reap what he has sown. It takes a Scoutmaster to reap what someone else has sown.

91

JUDY   What do you mean?

BASIL   I mean that in less than an hour, you will be promising to love, honor and obey me for the rest of your mortal days. If you don't love me now . . . (*He looks at his watch*) . . . you'd better hurry up. If you don't honor me, you've got exactly forty-seven minutes to find a way of doing so. As for obedience, I believe in it utterly. You can't run a Scout pack without it. And you know the punishment we have for telling lies, I suppose? We pour cold water down your sleeve. (*To the* VICAR) Incidentally, I always use hot water in the summer.

JUDY (*Alarmed*)   Basil, I've never seen you like this.

BASIL   Probably you've only seen me under the influence, that's why. But when I'm sober, I'm different. I'm polite, mark you, but firm. And I demand a certain amount of interest in my work. Long hikes, a lot of sleeping under canvas, a lot of welfare work with the kids in the youth clubs, community singing, educational games and the like. I always dreamed of a wife who would throw herself as wholeheartedly into the Guide movement as I have thrown myself among the Scouts. How about it, Judy? It's a grand life!

LADY   Judy has always been an open-air girl in her way.

JUDY   Mummy, I might as well join Daddy in his tree.

LADY (*Firm*)   Judy, you have made your choice.

VICAR   And a very sensible choice it is. Now, Robert, do you intend to raise a family?

ROBERT (*Awkward*)   I suppose so.

VICAR   And are you ready for marriage, Helga?

HELGA   I think I have been ready for some time, Vicar.

VICAR   Helga, you come from foreign parts, a distant land, the land, I believe, of Ibsen and Strindberg.

HELGA   Strindberg was a Swede.

VICAR   Well, that just shows how far away it is. (*He begins to talk to* LADY FITZBUTTRESS *as though of an invalid whose fate is uncertain*) I suppose there is no chance— I mean—the head of the family as it were—will not be gratifying us with his presence?

LADY   He's still up his tree.

VICAR   Still. Has any effort been made to communicate with him?

LADY   Every effort has been made, Vicar. I have called him, cajoled, pleaded.

ROBERT   Mother even threw stones at him.

LADY   To attract his attention, Robert, not to dislodge him. Nothing has been of any avail.

VICAR   And what do the doctors say?

LADY   Professor Priestman went up on a ladder and had a chat with him. I can't imagine what went on up there, but now I read in the papers that the Professor has taken up residence in a tree of his own.

VICAR   Yes, yes, I read that, too. Most distressing.

LADY   The Army sent their own psychiatrist, but unfortunately he had a morbid fear of heights and refused to go up the tree.

VICAR   Isn't that the man who has begun to live in a well?

LADY   Yes. It's too degrading, this sudden power of my husband's.

VICAR   Well, all the more reason for you to cling on to the norms of decent behavior. The ship may have lost its captain, let it not be said that it has lost its crew! Now I think the time has come for us to gird up our loins, as it were . . .
    (TINY *enters from the garden*)

LADY   Tiny, what are you doing here?

TINY   The decent thing, Doris. I have come to stand beside you, since Tubby won't.

VICAR   How very gracious, Brigadier.

TINY   A friend in need is a friend indeed. After all, that's what religion is all about, isn't it?

LADY   Tiny, I don't think . . .

TINY   Besides, Lady Fitzbuttress deserves a man by her side the day her two only children get married. Well, Robert, you look better with a haircut.

ROBERT   How's Paul?

TINY   The young are hardly remarkable for their tact, are they?

JUDY   How's your charming wife?

LADY   She's . . . not been too well lately, I understand.

ROBERT   Well, shouldn't we leave, Vicar, and get the business of the day over?

VICAR   I hardly think . . .

TINY   That's no way to talk, Robert, about the most solemn moment of your life.

ROBERT   It's my business to decide which is the most solemn moment of my life, and I'm not at all sold on you coming to my wedding.

LADY   Robert!

95

ROBERT It's me getting married—me and one or two others—no one else. If Dad felt like coming . . .

TINY Your father shows no sign of being able to understand what is going on. I've been watching him through my military binoculars. It's not a pretty sight.

LADY What do you mean?

TINY (*Suffering*) Don't force me to reply, Doris.

ROBERT Well, I'd rather him off his rocker, than you in your right mind.

TINY By George, you wouldn't talk to me like that if you were my son.

ROBERT I'd probably be in prison with my brother!

TINY Take that back! (*The* GENERAL *enters*) What are you doing here?

GENERAL What am I doing here? I've been listening behind the door.

TINY Ha! Eavesdropping?

GENERAL That's how we beat the Japanese, remember? Cracked their codes, listened in on their field telephones, forestalled their every move. I heard your celestial bicycle bell, Vicar—and then I saw the Brigadier in the distance setting out across the beet field in his morning suit. I guessed that something was up if the clan was gathering.

I shinnied down the tree and was in time to hear the most edifying lecture from the Vicar on the joys of marriage. Ah, Vicar, if only we had had such advice.

VICAR   You are not serious?

GENERAL   No, I am not; dear fellow, it was a paean to human gullibility, a hymn to hypocrisy, and I loved every minute of it. I particularly enjoyed the remark about the soft drink. Now let me see if my children were equally impressed. Robert—this is not a concession, is it? You're doing what you want to do, are you? Not merely to please me?

ROBERT   I am not thinking about you for a moment, Dad. I'm doing what I want to do.

GENERAL   You're sure? Helga?

HELGA   It's difficult to answer such a question, General. We wouldn't be here at all if we didn't want to go through with this.

ROBERT   Oh, people in love can live together . . . they don't have to get married if they're sincere, and honest . . . but it's somehow satisfying to make a gift of yourself . . . in front of witnesses.

GENERAL   That sounds like something I should be telling you.

ROBERT (*Shrugging*)   I only know it's something we had to find out for ourselves.

HELGA   Yeah. It would have been no use telling us.
(*The* GENERAL *nods agreement*)

JUDY   Dad, you haven't met Basil.

GENERAL   Basil . . .

BASIL   Basil Utterwood.

GENERAL   Utterwood? One of the Yorkshire Utterwoods?

BASIL   No, sir.

GENERAL   Oh, what a relief. (*Pulling* JUDY *aside*) Now,
my darling, you're not getting married for the reasons we
discussed . . . you remember?

JUDY   I don't know what you mean.

GENERAL   I mean . . . it must be awfully difficult being
a girl . . . nature won't allow you to forget your silliest
mistakes.

JUDY   Daddy. I'm not doing this for Andrew any more than
I'm doing it for myself. I want to get married, that's all. I'm
very happy.

GENERAL   My daughter seems so keen on marriage. I hope
she's equally keen on you.

BASIL   I think I understand her motives, sir.

GENERAL   Yes, but is that sufficient?

BASIL   Yes, sir.
(*They shake hands*)

GENERAL   My boy . . .

VICAR   If you're thinking of coming to the wedding, you really must change now, Sir Mallalieu.

GENERAL   What?

VICAR   A dark suit . . .

GENERAL   I'm not thinking of coming to the wedding, Vicar. I have outgrown your church.

VICAR   Outgrown my church . . . ?

GENERAL   . . . only in the sense a tree may be said to have outgrown the earth.

ROBERT   Oh, come along, Dad.

GENERAL   It's not a few minutes of mumbo-jumbo, Bob. It's what happens afterward that counts. All right, Vicar, take them away! I'm satisfied.

TINY   Mumbo-jumbo? I don't think you ought to talk that way about the sacrament of marriage.

GENERAL   What have you done with Daisy? Shot her?

LADY   Tubby . .

TINY   Hit me below the belt, would you? I'm not one to tell tales out of school, but if you provoke me . . .

GENERAL   What are you going to tell them, Tiny? Of how you broke my guitar at the regimental dinner?

LADY (*Outcry*)   Broke your guitar?

GENERAL   String by string—I've never seen such hatred lavished on a defenseless instrument. Had me arrested for breach of the peace. Gave evidence against me before the magistrate. Said I neglected my wife and children.

LADY   What possessed you, Tiny?

TINY   I won't allow you to think ill of me, Doris. I'll show you who is hypocritical—and I'll tell you my motives for coming here today—pure as the driven snow they are! Mallalieu's got a woman up his tree!

ALL (*Outcry*)   A woman!

GENERAL   Yes. It's Lesley. I found her drenched and pitiful on the lawn. I nursed her through pneumonia.

ROBERT (*Conscience-stricken*)   How is she?

GENERAL   She's much better, Bob—she's lost her voice.

TINY   Aren't you going to explain your behavior?

GENERAL   Oh, Tiny, I wish you hadn't come here.

TINY   I can well imagine that, you unutterable bounder. Perhaps you and I had better step outside for a moment.

GENERAL   Dear, silly old Tiny. That's why you never became a general, you see. Always threw in your reserves too soon. Take them off to church, Vicar, before I'm compelled to say some things I have never said before.

LADY (*Getting the message*)   Please go away, Tiny.

TINY   No, I won't go away, Doris. I have more right to be by your side than this madman.

VICAR   Are there some things I should know? What are your real motives in coming here today, Brigadier?

TINY   Good God, Vicar!

VICAR   There is no need to blaspheme!

TINY   Good grief, Vicar. There has been a vacancy beside Doris for so long.

VICAR   And a vacancy beside Mrs. Gilliat-Brown, also, I believe. Lady Fitzbuttress, have you anything to say?

LADY   No, I have not.

VICAR   It is curious . .

LADY   Please let me finish, Vicar. Tiny and Daisy are among our oldest friends. We used to play mixed doubles when we were younger. Ever since Mallalieu went up his tree, Tiny has gone out of his way to be kind and helpful to me.

VICAR Meanwhile leaving his own wife. It's a slightly inconsistent sense of honor, isn't it?

TINY (*Flabbergasted*) Inconsistent? Doris, is that the thanks I get for twenty-six years of patient and doglike waiting? Mixed doubles! An inadequate, misleading statement—an insult to my love for you.

LADY Don't be ridiculous, Tiny!

GENERAL (*Sotto voce*) Poor old Tiny. Now you've done it.

VICAR You have loved Lady Fitzbuttress for twenty-six years?

TINY Yes! And I love her more than ever today!

LADY My husband knows all about it. We used to laugh about it; didn't we, Mal?

GENERAL Don't be cruel, Doris.

VICAR You used to laugh about it?

LADY It was so stupid. Tiny was like a child. He used to hang around me and try to profit from Mallalieu's absence in such an infantile way. There was one time in Torquay . . .

TINY Don't dare desecrate the memory of Torquay!

LADY   But I never thought of giving myself to him. It would have been absolutely unthinkable.

TINY   That's a lie!

LADY   Tiny! Kindly leave the house!

TINY   That's a downright rotten lie, and you know it, Doris! And I don't believe Mallalieu ever knew! You never knew, did you? Did you?

GENERAL   All right, Doris, you've asked for it. I didn't want to come down from my tree and involve myself in all this painful history. Robert won't mind.

ROBERT   Won't mind what, Father?

LADY   Mallalieu, you're mad!

GENERAL   Helga won't mind either, because she's generous. I don't think it really concerns Judy . . .

LADY   Shouldn't we be off to church now, Vicar?

GENERAL   The fact is, Robert was born eleven months after I had been taken a prisoner of war.

LADY   Tubby, you brute.

TINY   (*Showing sudden paternity*)   Robert!

GENERAL   (*Stops* TINY)   I'm sorry, old man, we were captured the same day, remember?

TINY   You mean . . .

GENERAL   I had perhaps slightly more reason to count the months than you.

TINY   Robert's not even mine.

ROBERT   Who am I, then?

GENERAL   Have I misjudged you? I didn't think you'd care.

ROBERT   (*Looks at both men. To* LADY FITZBUTTRESS) Who's my father?

LADY   I'm too upset to reply. Let me get over what your father just said to me.

ROBERT   Which father?

LADY   Any father. Robert, do leave me alone.

TINY   Doris . . .

LADY   Tiny, get out of my way!

GENERAL   Well?

ROBERT   Well? What difference does it make? I may have lost a father . . . two fathers even . . . but I've acquired a wife. I think I've come out of it jolly well.

GENERAL   D'you mean that?

ROBERT   Of course I do.

GENERAL   Good boy!

ROBERT   You thought I'd be upset, otherwise you'd never have bothered to say you thought I wouldn't care. What you don't understand is—I really *don't* care.

GENERAL   That's unnatural, son. You must care a little.

ROBERT   Why? I've never thought blood was much of a tie compared to love and compassion. We'd all be much better off if we could choose our relatives as we choose our wives. (*After a moment*) I might even have chosen you if I'd known sooner that you weren't my father.

GENERAL   I wonder, Bob. Aren't you just saying that to be kind?

ROBERT   You didn't make it easy for me . . . I suppose you know that.

GENERAL   Nothing worth doing is easy.

ROBERT   You could have destroyed a lesser fellow.

GENERAL   You're not a lesser fellow.

ROBERT   How did you know that?

GENERAL   Took a chance on it.

ROBERT   You haven't changed a single one of my ideas. You realize that?

GENERAL Good.

ROBERT The fact that I cut my hair means nothing. If they call on me to fight, I still won't go. I'll just say no— politely.

GENERAL I don't care what you do, Robert, so long as you are yourself, not a type. That's what I was when I came home to retire. I wasn't myself. I was just some kind of General. And you weren't yourself either. You were some sort of General's son.

ROBERT You know, it's rather exciting not knowing who my father is. The possibilities are enormous. He might have been a great murderer, or an embezzler . . . or even a stockbroker!

GENERAL Stockbroker, Doris? No, your mother always had rather conservative tastes. And then, she possessed a king of collective fidelity, an esprit de corps. I'm dreadfully afraid your father will turn out to be yet another officer in the regiment.

HELGA Robert, our child won't have much luck, will it? To know exactly who its father is? What a dull start to life.

VICAR What a what?

HELGA What a dull start to . . .

VICAR Forgive me if I'm a little slow-witted, but I find myself absolutely unable to follow this conversation. Did I understand that you are expecting a child, Helga?

GENERAL   Great scot, Vicar! Surely you don't have to be told that. Just look at her.

HELGA   He said I'd eaten too much butter.

GENERAL   (*Delighted*)   You call that butter, do you?

VICAR   My suspicions about Helga's condition were aroused after my inadvertent remark about farmhouse butter, not before.

GENERAL   The fact is that even after your suspicions were aroused, you decided it was safer not to ask questions until you were driven to it. Do you wish to ask anything of Judy? Judy!

JUDY   What?

VICAR   No, I have no questions to ask.

GENERAL   Well, I have. Utterwood. Do you consider yourself the father of young Andrew?

BASIL   Do I consider myself the father? Yes, I do.

GENERAL   But *are* you?

BASIL   That hardly matters, does it?

JUDY   He *is!*

BASIL   Hold these for a moment, will you? (*He takes a vase from the bench and gives* JUDY *the flowers from it*) You,

Judy . . . (*He pours water down her arm*) really oughtn't
to fib.

JUDY   Oh. You beast, you've ruined my dress!

BASIL   I never thought for a moment I was the father of that
child, but I was very flattered that anybody should think
I could be . . . you see, away from the campfire and the
sing-song, I am a shy man . . . even as a miler, I never
seem to come in first, because I hate to disappoint the other
runners . . . I don't have the kind of confidence it takes
to assess my own worth and pit it against other people.

GENERAL   (*Alarmed*)   But are you sure you want to go
through with it in that case, Utterwood? Judy's a tough
proposition for anyone . . .

BASIL   It's a question of temperament, Sir Mallalieu. I
wasn't at all interested in Judy until I was sure she was
lying.

JUDY   I wasn't lying.

BASIL   (*Pouring water down her other arm*)   I hate to be lied
to, but on the other hand, I have to feel I'm needed. I'm
very conscious of my bank account with God, and I like
to have a reserve. Besides, I think I can make something
out of Judy. A girl who can lie so conscientiously in order
to give her baby a domestic life can't be *all* bad. Oh, it
won't be easy. She'll hang back at first, because she's
mentally idle and physically self-indulgent, but I'm sure
that with buckets of cold water, a lot of exercise and a
modicum of prayer, we'll make a full life for her yet. And,

in return, who knows, she may even teach me to win the mile. (*The baby cries*) It's all right, old girl. I'll get it. (*He sprints up the stairs*)

GENERAL   Judy, why on earth didn't you find him earlier?

JUDY   You mean you like him?

GENERAL   He's one of the few really good men I've ever met. You're so much nicer than you allow yourself to be . . . you are, darling, you know . . . go and get ready! (*She runs off*) By George, they're splendid, splendid, aren't they, Vicar?

VICAR   Who is splendid?

GENERAL   The young people. I never guessed they had it in them. Even Judy. Did you see how she looked at me just then? Like a little Madonna. She's in love too.

VICAR   We all have our own concept of little Madonnas, Sir Mallalieu. No, I'm sorry, Sir Mallalieu. I have seen nothing admirable, nothing in the youth today. They are a depraved and undisciplined lot.

GENERAL   Are you as blind as that? Is it possible? Vicar, if Christ returned today, he would cull his first disciples from among the young, because they would consider a second coming the most natural thing in the world. Only we would regard it with suspicion, and ask for proof, despite the evidence.

VICAR   You are not seriously comparing the young to the disciples of old . . .

GENERAL   Not yet, no. They are still experimenting with right and wrong, and ruining their health trying to find short cuts to apocalyptic vision, but they are unashamed in their quest for love and gentleness, which is more than can be said for us! I would readily compare us to the Pharisees.

VICAR   That is most generous of you, I'm sure!

GENERAL (*Ferocious*)   Vicar, the young are infinitely purer of mind than we.

VICAR   That again is a matter of opinion.

TINY   Who was it, Doris? Clive Clayton-Mallowes, I bet.

LADY   I'll never forgive you, Tiny, for what you did today.

TINY   Don't rub salt in the wound. You've bloody well broken my heart, that's what you've done.

LADY   Is that so? Well, I'm glad!

TINY (*Shouting*)   Glad!

GENERAL (*Gallantly, conciliatory*)   She didn't mean it, Tiny.

LADY   I mean every word I say. Tiny has made my life a nightmare for the last twenty-six years with his constant attentions and his jealousy.

TINY   I never cared for Clayton-Mallowes.

LADY   And you're no better, with your sarcasm, and your immorality, and your tree. Poor Lesley, up there. You and Tiny deserve each other. Why don't you go off together and spend the rest of your life in some club? You know nothing about women, either of you!

VICAR   Lady Fitzbuttress!

LADY (*Suddenly all charm*)   Vicar! I quite forgot you were there. I'll be in my room, in case either of you feels like apologizing.
            (*She goes*)

VICAR (*Spiritually exhausted*)   I'm sorry, Sir Mallalieu, the camel's back is broken. I just can't see my way to going through with this ceremony.

GENERAL   Oh, Vicar, now don't you collapse on me! For years you have judged by appearances, and you would have been content to do so today if I hadn't had the absurd idea of coming down from my tree. They'd have been on their way to church by now, creamery butter and all, with you none the wiser. What a fool I was!

VICAR   I am glad you came down, Sir Mallalieu.

GENERAL (*No nonsense*)   Well, you can't have it both ways, Vicar. Ever since I've known you, my wife and I, Brigadier Gilliatt-Brown *and* Daisy, have been regular churchgoers. Daisy was pretty peculiar, even then. Can you be sure that similar skeletons don't reside peacefully in the cupboards of most of your congregation?

VICAR   Oh no, it just isn't possible.

GENERAL   You didn't think it possible of us an hour ago.

VICAR (*Soul searching*)   Well, I must say, I always noticed that Mrs. Gilliatt-Brown failed to rise for the hymns, and she had a habit of falling to her knees well before the invocation to prayer. I put it down to an intensely personal religious experience. It had never occurred to me before today . .

GENERAL   Exactly! Now Vicar, how much do you really know of what goes on around you? How much do any of us know? Give us the benefit of your doubt.

VICAR   No, I cannot, Sir Mallalieu. You have made yourself public property. My clemency may be misinterpreted.

GENERAL   What do you mean?

VICAR   You must know that all over England, distinguished men are following your example. The papers are full of it. The tendency is quickly taking the form of a national emergency.

GENERAL   I had no idea. I don't get the papers up in the tree, you know.

VICAR   A member of the Cabinet went up only yesterday morning, and has refused the exhortation of the Prime Minister to come down and vote. That is bad enough, Sir Mallalieu, but when it becomes known that you have a woman up there with you, I shudder to think of the re-percussions.

GENERAL Vicar, you're exaggerating. My woman, as you call her, is only Lesley . . . I could never explain that to you . . . but like you, I judged by appearances. I was very rude to her once down here. I woefully misjudged her. She'll be on her way sooner or later, but she'll have taught me something which I could have only learned in the treetops. With any luck I'll have taught her something too.

VICAR And what is that?

GENERAL Respect for all things.

VICAR (*Ironic*) Respect?

GENERAL Have you ever been up a tree, Vicar?

VICAR Not since my extreme youth.

GENERAL But your aim then was probably to bring some-thing down. A kite or a lost ball.

VICAR (*Ashamed*) Apples.

GENERAL Apples? Your own?

VICAR No.

GENERAL Well, a fine tree is a miracle of proportion, Vicar —and a sense of proportion is its gift to its inhabitant. Men

and their problems are cut down to size, while the sky seems strangely intimate and accessible. You should try it sometime.
(LADY FITZBUTTRESS *enters*)

LADY   The last thing I want to do is interrupt your tête-à-tête, but I believe it is time to leave for the church.

VICAR (*Consulting his watch*)   Good lack! The ceremony is due to begin in eleven minutes.

LADY   Children! Children! We're off!
(ROBERT *and* HELGA *enter*)

VICAR   Come along now, come along.
(BASIL *enters down the stairs with the baby in his arms;* JUDY *follows*)

BASIL   Oh, are we off? What shall we do with Andrew? He's in a playful mood. We'd better take him along with us.

VICAR   Certainly not.

TINY (*Glum*)   I'll look after him.

VICAR   You don't insist on accompanying us, then?

TINY   I wouldn't dream of it.

LADY   Well, that's a relief.

ROBERT Dad, if you need anything, don't bother to come down in the future—Helga or I'll bring it to you.

HELGA And Robert can play you a piece on his guitar.

GENERAL Oh, you've learned to play it, have you?

ROBERT Yes. I have. It's a different tune than yours, of course.

GENERAL Of course.
 (*They all file out*)

VICAR Come on, all of you. Smiles. Smiles. Remember, this is a joyous occasion. There will be spectators and there will be Press. Try to hold yourself in, Helga.
 (*They all leave except the* VICAR *and* LADY FITZ-BUTTRESS)

LADY Your room is always ready, Mal, should you ever change your mind.

GENERAL Yes—and I've got a nice, low branch prepared for you, Doris, should you ever change yours.
 (LADY FITZBUTTRESS *leaves*)

VICAR One final question, Sir Mallalieu.

GENERAL Yes?

VICAR Does the tree have to be of a certain height, or will any tree do?

GENERAL   The height of the tree is in the mind, Vicar.

VICAR (*Interested*)   In the mind, is it? Yes . . .

LADY (*Offstage*)   Vicar!

VICAR   Coming. Yes.
     (*He exits*)

TINY (*Holding the baby; he is alone with the* GENERAL)   I want to apologize, Tubby.

GENERAL   Oh, don't bother, Tiny.

TINY   It's just that . . . I'm an emotional kind of fellow, in spite of appearances . . . all my life, I've stuck my neck out . . . and somehow, I always end up holding the baby.

GENERAL   Yes.

TINY (*Rises*)   I was going to ask you . . .

GENERAL   Mm?

TINY   Would there be room for one more up your tree?

GENERAL   Of course, old man. But you know, Tiny, it has no future, however enthusiastic I may sound. We've come too far into the quagmire. I'm spoiled. There are things I miss up there, even if I pretend it's perfect. I miss the activity. I miss the confusion . . . the imperfection. I miss

116

my whiskey and my newspapers. However high you go, you're still only halfway up the tree.

TINY (*Alarmed*) Look here, you've got to stay up there, Tubby. Robert and Helga said they would bring you up anything you want. I'll arrange to have a half a bottle of Scotch and a copy of the *Times* at the foot of the tree every morning—that'll be my contribution. A soda syphon, as well . . . and I'll replace that banjo I broke. Anything within my power. But you've simply got to stay up there.

GENERAL (*Sadly*) That's what happens when you find freedom on this earth, Tiny. Before you know it, it's turned into another prison. Every day would be like Christmas. I'd wake up every morning wondering what presents I'll find at the bottom of the tree.

TINY You're a leader, Tubby, I'm not. That's the price a leader has to pay. Even if you're only halfway up the tree, old boy, you owe it to us to pretend you're at the top. We're looking to you, Tubby. We need you up there.

GENERAL I'd like to keep an eye on the young people.

TINY Paul's getting out of prison next week. I'd like to be up the tree before he comes home. Do him a world of good to feel he's on his own.

GENERAL (*Nods slowly*) Very well. Recreation's over. Back to work.

TINY Yes, Tubby. When do I report to the tree?

GENERAL   Let me see. I've got to give Lesley her geometry
lesson. When the sun is halfway between its zenith and
the horizon.

TINY   Promise me it's not too late.

GENERAL   Often too early—never too late.

TINY (*Enthusiastic*)   Very good, Tubby. And what if it
rains?

GENERAL   It won't rain.

TINY   Thanks, Tubby. That's the stuff we've all been waiting for.
(*The* GENERAL *salutes absently*)

GENERAL (*As he leaves*)   Carry on.
(*We hear wedding bells*)

Curtain